Real l

"The last time I worked with Renée, I told her exactly what my goals were and when I wanted to achieve them. She sent me the perfect plan to help me reach my goals. I followed her instructions down to the letter, and I was able to get the results I wanted. These results meant that when I went to Hawaii for vacation, I was comfortable and confident enough to wear a bikini in public for the first time in my life!" – Kelsey L.

"Renée has been a strong motivator and ally in my continued effort to improve my health. She's great at creating programs that work for you, considering the time you have, and the goals you want to achieve. She's honest, positive, encouraging, and just generally one of the kindest people you'll have the opportunity to meet. Even if we haven't worked together in some time, I know she's always a call, text, or email away." – Melissa C.

"The first day I met Renée, I felt instantly comfortable. After listening to all of my concerns and goals, she thoughtfully developed a personalized plan for me that delivered jaw-dropping results after just 90 short days! Renée's expertise delivers results! To this day, she always responds to all of my questions in a thorough and supportive way." – Wendy M.

"Renée emphasizes proper form and is action-based; she's not just going through the motions. I have the utmost respect for her and her profession. She treats everyone with respect. Renée really should have representation. She is the epitome of a fit female athlete." – Dawn M.

"Renee goes above and beyond coaching you to reach your goals (without the gimmicks or the "quick fixes"), and she genuinely cares about helping you attain and maintain your goals. Working with Renée has truly been a great experience for me. She is different than any other personal trainer I have worked with – she lives a fitness lifestyle and leads by example – and focuses on long-term sustainable goals." – Loni C.

"For years, I had been doing the same workout, hoping to get results. It wasn't until I met and began working with Renée in both group and private one-on-one training sessions that I truly began to see improvement and have fun! Renée has helped me create a more balanced nutrition plan. With her in my corner, I know I'm just starting to scratch the surface of what I can and will accomplish." – Melinda F.

"Renée's guidance and understanding are invaluable to me. She is a coach who truly listens, cares, and works with your specific needs. Renée has an amazing gift of making people feel special." – Edith S.

"Renée encourages me when I am struggling, challenges me when I need it, and always helps me stay focused on my goals." – Deanna C.

"Renée is very thoughtful with the nutritional "training" aspect and incorporates a nutrition plan that is satisfying and not overly restrictive, resulting in a long-term sustainable and healthier lifestyle. Renée taught me how to make better choices with wholesome, fulfilling foods combined with exercise for a healthier lifestyle, instead of focusing on negativity and "starving" myself to try to reach a certain look or goal weight." – Anna T.

Ditch the fads and body battles.
Regain your focus, get fit, and
feel like your true self again.

Feel Good Again

RENÉE MACGREGOR, PNC-MHC, CPPC
Leading Expert in Total Body Transformations

The information contained within this book is not intended to serve as a replacement for medical advice. It is strongly recommended that individuals consult with a qualified healthcare professional concerning matters pertaining to their health, particularly those that may require diagnosis or medical intervention. The author and publisher explicitly disclaim any responsibility for any liability, loss, or risk, whether personal or otherwise, resulting directly or indirectly from the utilization or application of any material within this book.

This document is a nonfictional work. However, it is important to note that the names and personal attributes of the individuals involved have been altered with the intent to preserve their anonymity. Any similarity to individuals, whether living or deceased, or to their situations, is purely coincidental and entirely unintended.

ISBN: 979-8-218-34092-6
Edited by: Bonita Jewel and Jennifer Collins

Printed in the United States of America

Dedication

To my parents, thank you for your love and guidance.
I am the driven person I am today because of you.

To my big brother, for being one of my biggest supporters
since we were little. You were my first best friend.

For my love. Thank you for always believing in me.
You have my heart. You always will.

To everyone who has ever supported and believed in me,
I truly appreciate you. More than you know.

Check out these expert-guided options and wellness freebies all on ReneeMacGregor.com!

Join the Weight Loss Community:

Private One-on-One Opportunities:

FREE Downloads at reneemacgregor.com:

Renée MacGregor

Contents

A Note to the Reader

A story is a precious gift that offers insight into the commonalities we all share. Stories resonate with us because we relate to them. Within this book, we will find aspects of our own story within the stories of other women. In reading stories, introspection is manifested; we look within and discover more about ourselves. As this process of self-discovery continues, influenced by the experiences of other women, we can then take proper action steps that will lead to personal fulfillment.

While the stories you'll read in this book are about real women, I have changed my clients' names and some minor details to protect privacy. To all of you who have blessed this book with your experiences, I am profoundly grateful. My wholehearted goal is to honor these women by empowering others.

This book focuses on real women's experiences, but also offers you transformative activities that will allow you to discover your vision, mission, and goals, as well as to better understand yourself by recognizing what is deeply meaningful to you. It provides guidance on how to conquer your harmful habits, hormones, and transform your body once and for all.

These activities may be written out on a normal sheet of paper, or use my *free* workbook download that is provided for you on my website:

https://reneemacgregor.com/product/feel-good-again-workbook

Introduction

Life is full of extraordinary moments that we often overlook. We tend to forget how much a complete miracle and blessing life is.

There is absolutely nothing *more* important in your life than your health. Nothing. I know you may be thinking, "No, my kids are definitely more important ..."

Even if you are a parent, *your* health is more important.

Why? If you don't take care of your health, you might not be around for your children when they need you most, or available to experience their proudest moments. If you are not healthy, your ability to help, support, and care for others is impacted.

So, let's talk about health.

One factor of health, and the one which people generally have the most control over, is weight.

In our modern American culture, we're seeing a disturbing trend in the area of health and fitness: obesity. More people in the U.S. are overweight, dangerously overweight, or morbidly obese than at any other time in history. Based on data from a survey conducted by the CDC in 2020, 42% of U.S. adults are obese and 9.2% are severely obese.[1]

For U.S. adults 20-39 years of age, the obesity rate is at 39.8%. Obesity is highest among U.S. adults 40-59 years of age (44.3%) and only slightly lower in the 60+ age range (41.5%).[1] These statistics came out right as the first COVID-19 lockdowns were happening. Imagine what they are today, post-pandemic!

In order to prevent ourselves from becoming including in these statistics, or to remove ourselves from being a part of them, we must try to strive for a healthier future.

You may be someone who wants to shed extra weight but hasn't had success yet. That's okay. We've *all* had times where we've been unsuccessful at something. That *does not* make us failures.

Everyone who starts something new experiences times of being uncomfortable, falling short, or even making mistakes; yet, they can still learn, grow, and become stronger *because* of that.

You have the potential to get stronger *because* of your past.

Right now, I want you to embrace this book as evidence that you are *getting stronger!* By reading this book, you show that you are pressing forward despite what may not have worked in the past, despite the things other people might have said to you, despite the hurt you have experienced or are still going through.

You want to live a long and healthy life, but you haven't fully figured out how to do that effectively.

That is what this book will show you.

Like many human beings, I have experienced health issues, hormone imbalances, injuries, losses, and challenges, that I have had to overcome. It's in these experiences that I have grown the most through objective self-reflection, self-analysis, self-discovery, and applying positive behavior modification.

I have lived a health-focused mindset for almost thirty years. Along the way, I experienced highs and lows, phases of laser focus and loss of focus, but my internal motivations have always been a driving force.

Living a life striving for optimal health is a personal passion of mine that constantly motivates me, but more importantly, it's a way to help others achieve their optimal health by sharing what I have learned over the decades.

I am a full-time Certified Master Health Coach, certified in Nutrition, Change Psychology, Prenatal and Postnatal Coaching, a Fitness Coach, and an expert in exercise biomechanics. My many years of experience with clients has blessed me with a wealth of knowledge and hands-on experience. Using my expertise, I have coached clients privately in a one-on-one setting and in a group setting, both in-person and remotely, locally and nationwide.

It's my life's mission to help as many people as I can to learn the fundamentals of living and maintaining a healthy lifestyle by guiding them towards success and independence. Every individual I mentor is unique and at a different point in their health journey, but they all have the power to succeed with the proper guidance.

Despite whatever feelings you are experiencing, you are in this moment for a reason. So, embrace who you are today with open arms. This book will help you better understand the most unique nuances of you that make you ... *you.*

Your story is still unwritten, and you have a path to walk.

You may not yet have accepted that your health is the first priority in your life, and that's okay.

For now, let's work on transforming how we *think* about becoming healthy in order to chart a path toward achieving our ultimate goals!

It starts from within.

Part 1

Connecting to Internal Motivation

If you don't have in mind a meaningful reason for becoming healthy, then the path to success becomes much, much tougher.

Too often, we're motivated by things people say to us or how we think others perceive us. Someone you haven't seen for a while makes a comment about how form-fitting those jeans are, and all of a sudden, you're browsing Amazon for weight loss pills.

But those impulses rarely last long.

In order to properly attach meaning to why you want to get healthy, you need to understand your own purpose.

The "why" of it all.

Nothing is more powerful than internal motivation.

Some examples of meaningful internal motivations include getting healthy to be a positive role model for your children, to be able to provide better care for someone else, to live longer and become a grandparent, or staying healthy to pursue a career you are passionate about until you can retire later in life.

When you're able to shift that external motivation to something internal, something deeply meaningful to you ... Wow, look out! You cannot lose.

My hope is that you will absorb this book, like vitamins and minerals, into your body. Allow yourself to dive deep into the stories of other women whose lives were changed forever with a little guidance. These stories showcase commonalities we all share, which creates a deeper understanding of our situations and that we are not alone.

If you read this with an open heart and mind and complete the self-discovery activities, your internal motivation will be revealed. You will be empowered and ready to create success; and find your inner peace.

You are fully capable of achieving everything you have ever wanted. You *deserve* to live the healthy, vibrant, and energized life you have been searching for.

This is a journey that leads you to a place of true happiness, confidence, and healthy living.

Self-reflection is the key to understanding your uniqueness and to truly knowing who you are today. So many times, I've witnessed family, friends, and clients reach a point where they realized they didn't truly know who they were. They were moving through life on autopilot, doing what they assumed other people expected them to do or what they thought was just the "next step" in life when, in fact, they were losing themselves a little bit along the way.

They struggled to sleep at night, felt worried or stressed, and wondered why they were unsettled and disconnected from their real purpose in life.

In working with dozens of people like this, I realized how important self-discovery, internal motivation and purpose are, leading me to write this book. *Feel Good Again* is designed to take you to a place of self-discovery and provide purposeful guidance on how to achieve anything that is deeply meaningful to you.

You can truly achieve *anything*, no matter what it is! Whether it is losing weight, getting fit, changing your career, or finding true happiness, once you truly understand what is deeply meaningful to you, the doorways to possibility open and you can step through with confidence.

But, first, you must understand your life and what makes you truly unique and amazing.

This book will invite you to self-reflect on a deeper level, so you can critically think about what action steps you need to create in order to succeed in your journey toward sustainably healthy living.

This book is the "think" before you "do" ... the "walk before you run." If you have certain goals you want to start tackling, then ideally, you'll first complete working through this book and the exercises included here to ensure your success.

These pages will provide you with the expert knowledge to change your life. But let's be real. Anything that is positively life-changing will take effort. And if you are *truly ready* for this process, this will excite you, not discourage you.

You have the choice to complete the exercises, but only the readers who thoughtfully complete these activities will take advantage of this book's full potential.

Why? Because there's a true link between active learning and long-lasting success.

The Learning Pyramid was researched and created by the National Training Laboratories.[2] It illustrates learner recall percentages based on different approaches, indicating that active learning leads to a much higher retention rate than passive learning. Retention is key to creating long-term change and transforming your body.

This is why I strongly encourage you to embrace the opportunity to do more than just passively read. Completing the Self-Discovery activities within this book is important. It will be up to you whether you want to demonstrate your learning, start a book discussion group, teach others, or immediately put into practice what you have learned.

After reading this book and participating in the exercises, you will have found clarity regarding your true self, and your deeply meaningful purpose and goals. And you will be able to apply this clarity and purpose to your everyday life.

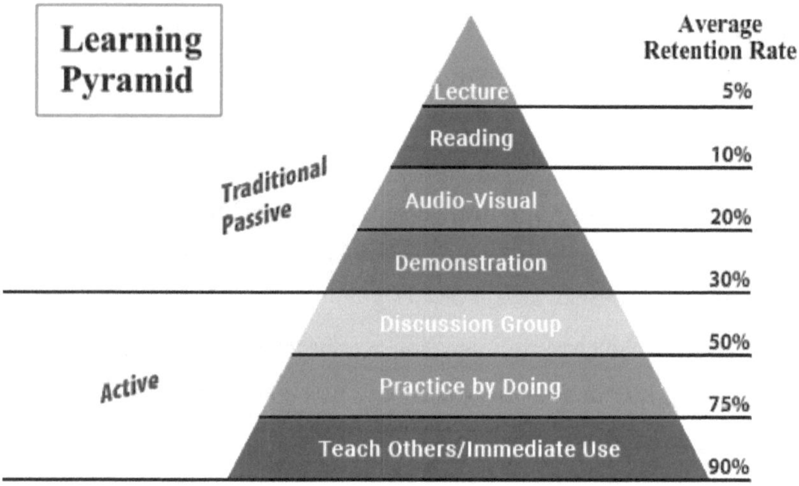

Source: National Training Laboratories, Bethel, Maine

Meanwhile, I will be your initial guide on this journey.

I say "initial" because, in every stage of our lives, there are many people who contribute to our "awakenings," our improvements, and our evolutions. These people are often referred to as mentors or guides.

It's important to know your guide because a person's life is built on the foundation of their experiences, successes and mistakes, supporters and critics, and so much more. When we are talking about your health and fitness, we are talking about a lot more than simply what you eat, how often you exercise, and how sedentary your work life has become.

Your guide's principles and objectives should resonate with you and support your life and mission.

Wherever you are at this stage in your life – whatever age, health status, history, and traits that embody you – I want to formally welcome you to this incredible journey of self-discovery, limitless possibility, and self-empowerment for the betterment of your future.

I have the utmost respect for you because you are taking the initial steps in your journey. As you travel through this book, we will take that journey together.

So, I invite you to learn a little about me.

My Story

Have you ever felt as though you "lost" yourself?

At one time, you were so certain about who you were and where you were going, but then a few months or years later, you found yourself staring at a reflection you didn't fully recognize anymore, and wondered, *What am I doing? Who am I?*

I totally get it.

Like most people, my life has been an evolution. Sometimes, the changes I faced were small and subtle. Other times were cataclysmic, massive earthquakes that completely altered the landscape of my life.

Having lived in California since I was a toddler, I know a thing or two about earthquakes. Every week, there are tiny seismic anomalies occurring under our feet. Most of them are so minor or so deep beneath the surface that we never notice them.

The ripple effects that come from earthquakes can cause lasting damage to a geographic landscape. The term for these effects is *ground surface deformation*, which often leads to permanent consequential changes in nearby areas.[3]

Life is like that, isn't it? Every day, you wake up and face challenges. Some familiar, some new, but always a few. Most of the time, we barely think twice about these minor events or how they shape and mold our lives, but over time, they do. The challenges we face impact our decisions, beliefs, hopes, fears, and every other component of our life.

These challenges, these changes, are the lights, the darks, and the grays that make each of us unique. I am no exception.

The incredible thing I have learned while venturing along this journey is that I didn't fully understand myself until I forced myself to ask the tough questions.

The Tough Questions

What are the tough questions?

- Who was I in the past?
- Who am I today?
- How has my relationship with my parents formed who I am today?
- What experiences in my life have been pivotal, and how can I learn from them?
- What interests and activities bring me joy?
- What do I *need* in a life partner? What do I *want*? What is a *dealbreaker* for me?
- What is the purpose of my life?
- How can I take the things I am passionate about and actually incorporate them into my purpose?

These are difficult questions, but important ones. People usually start to ask themselves questions like these when they look around and see an unfamiliar landscape – when they realize their life is not on the path they *assumed* it was or *thought* it should be on.

One day, I came to that point and found myself asking these tough questions of myself. What I discovered drove me to new chapters in my life. New challenges and new fulfillments.

I grew up in Northern California. My family dynamic included support, unconditional love, unforgettable fights, high expectations, spirituality, and wholesome meals. My relationship with my parents played a critical role in who I would become. The relationships you have with your parents, grandparents, and any parental role model in your life is the same. They influence us and, to some degree, help determine the people we become.

Most people may not recognize small, seemingly insignificant moments as being impactful until many years later when they look back. Maybe in looking back now, you can see some of these events that shaped you – parental approval, your high school graduation ceremony, a heartwarming moment during a childhood birthday, or something a teacher taught you.

These things linger with you to this day.

For me, one of my first positive, life-changing "tremors", happened as a teenager when my parents signed up the entire family for a gym membership. I wasn't a fitness buff and was not actively involved in sports. So stepping into that gym for the first time was surreal.

Those first few months were an exploratory phase.

Each passing week, I discovered there was a passion brewing within.

I wanted to test my limits. This is where the passion for physical fitness started and a "fire" was lit in me. It burns even brighter and stronger now.

And, today, that fire also drives a deeper purpose within me. A deeper meaning. *Healthy living is more than just exercise.*

When I was growing up, we didn't go out for dinner often. Eating out can get quite expensive, and it was viewed as a luxury for my family, which it is.

For us, it was simply a matter of practicality. With two kids in school and both parents working, eating out wasn't practical, especially on busy weekdays. Our eating style was what one may call a typical American diet. Breakfasts often consisted of cereal during the week, and usually the kind full of sugar. On weekends, my parents would often prepare eggs with a side of bacon or sausage, or delicious waffles or pancakes.

Lunch generally consisted of a bag lunch that my mom would make us. If I was lucky, I'd get to buy lunch at school – which was never healthy back then. When it wasn't a school day, lunch was typically a PBJ or turkey and cheese sandwich accompanied by a side of chips or crackers.

Dinnertime was different.

This was family time. No matter what was going on in our lives, this was the one time of the day where we all came together and everything seemed wholesome. Distractions weren't allowed at the table, either. Dinnertime was cherished as our means of staying connected. We enjoyed protein, plenty of vegetables, carbohydrates, and ice cream for dessert. All fairly wholesome, except the ice cream. To this day, dinnertime is still extremely important to me because I love my family and I want to stay connected to them.

As the years passed, and I grew up, I noticed my parents beginning to slowly gain weight.

In general, as people get older, they tend to become less physically active, which typically contributes to weight gain at varying degrees.

There was a time when my mother had lost a lot of weight running outdoors on a regular basis, but she gained it back. This is a pattern I've seen play out time and time again with many people: they find an exciting new exercise routine or regiment, or a fad diet plan, and they latch on. Some people don't stick with these for more than a few days while others lose weight, start to feel and look better, and gain their confidence back.

But what happens when their excitement for their new, healthy push wears off and they give up on it? Most of them gain all that weight back (more, in many cases).

For many years, my father and mother tried different weight loss plans with varying degrees of success, but they were always temporary. As they aged, the added weight brought on new health challenges, including joint pain, high blood pressure, sleep apnea, diabetes, and all of the frustration and annoyances that come along with carrying that extra weight around.

As an adult, I truly began to realize these health realities about my parents, I felt powerless. I *was* powerless. There is a difference between feeling powerless and helpless, and *knowing* that you are. We all know that you cannot change someone or force them to do things differently, even if it is a positive change.

Over the years, my worry for my parents increased – their health, their lives, and their future.

One morning, I was unloading dishes from the dishwasher before heading to work. Out of nowhere, I started sobbing uncontrollably. I know what you might be thinking: hormones. But it was not "that time of the month" for me. I started reflecting on various thoughts that had been on my mind in recent days and it took a few minutes for me to pinpoint why I was crying.

I began thinking about my parents and their health, and sadness and fear overwhelmed me. Up until that moment, I'd never realized how much stress I was carrying around when it came to worrying about my parents' health, knowing I was powerless.

Family is everything for many people, and we tend to love our families more than life itself. That subconscious worry and stress hit a breaking point for me that day. But I had to decide to let it go because I had no control over the actions my family members took, and the stress was only negatively affecting me.

This was one turning point in my life. I knew that if I couldn't help my parents, I wanted to try to help as many other people as I could. This was my mission.

Even today, though, I'll admit there are too many times when I still feel powerless. Why?

It's simple, really, and it is at the heart of what this book is all about. In my parents' example, they have all the information in the world at their disposal, and yet they still aren't making healthy decisions about their bodies and overall wellness.

Information does not cause transformation.

Even as I help guide my clients to a healthier outlook and way of life, some tend to go back to their unhealthy habits. Why? We will discuss this very soon.

My Life-changing Journey

In early May of 2008, less than a month before my first marriage started, I had what is referred to as an abnormal gynecological appointment. After my honeymoon, I spent nine months in a state of doubt and fear, waiting and hoping for some clarity, as well as some better understanding of what was happening with my body.

Every couple months, I was put through a barrage of tests with no clear answers. I felt guilty because all of these tests prevented me from giving my new husband the "honeymoon" phase he deserved.

I also worried for what my health concerns might mean for myself and for our future together, constantly allowing my imagination to run in all of the worst possible directions.

I spent months worrying, wondering, doubting, and stressing over the unknown. I senselessly put myself through so much unnecessary worry about something I knew nothing about. This reminds me of a quote from Michael J. Fox:

"Don't spend a lot of time imagining the worst-case scenario. It rarely goes down as you imagine it will, and if by some fluke it does, you will have lived it twice."

Such sound advice that I should have taken to heart.

Finally, in early 2009, my doctor walked into the room where I sat waiting. I remember her exact words: "This is now considered cervical cancer." The look on her face was one of empathy and genuine concern.

I was looking at the lab image she held in front of me. None of it made any sense to me. My doctor even tried to draw me a picture to better illustrate what the microscopic lab image was showing. Deep down, I was probably hoping to find something that would prove the diagnosis wrong.

But, strangely, while I sat listening to my doctor, I finally actually felt some measure of peace. For the first time, it was like a huge weight had been lifted off of my shoulders.

I finally had answers. All those months of worrying over the unknown had been cast aside. It's fascinating how the unknown can cause more stress and strain than the known.

While I was going over this diagnosis, an overwhelming sense of calm came over me. I thought to myself, *there's nothing I can do about this anymore.* My life was now in the hands of my doctors and God. God had carried me that far, and I knew he had a higher purpose for me. One that still wasn't clear to me.

A month later, I had a procedure called a Conization. This surgical procedure involves removing tissue in a cone shape from the cervix and cervical canal. Thankfully, because we had caught the cancer early, when it was still localized, surgery was optimal for stopping it in its tracks.

Recovery was not at all smooth or easy. There were many bumps along the way.

Unbeknownst to me, as my body had healed from the surgery, my cervix had nearly closed completely. Ladies, as you can imagine, this made it quite difficult for my menstrual cycle to run its course with ease. For almost five years, most of my cycles were unbearable. I'd experience extreme dysmenorrhea (menstrual cramps) due to my uterus contracting without being able to shed its lining to allow for the expulsion of menstrual blood.

In general, contractions are triggered by the release of chemicals called prostaglandins, which can cause inflammation and pain.[4] Several times, this pain was so severe that I had to be driven to the emergency room, only for them to tell me there was nothing they could do.

I remember one experience so vividly. At the time, I was working from home, and every 2-3 minutes, these excruciating contractions would hit me so badly that I would squirm in my chair and my lower back would feel like it was on fire! In this instance, I lived with this pain for thirteen hours before I finally "raised my white flag" of surrender and had my (now) ex-husband drive me to the emergency room.

Even in challenging times, I somehow always manage to have a little sense of humor. I told the ER Doctor, "There better be a baby in there!"

I did get him to laugh, but that was all he provided. No solutions. Just, "It's your body trying to push out your menstrual cycle."

That was just one example of many. Every month, when my body was attempting to shed its lining, it was like a tsunami where my entire cycle would happen in a matter of several hours ... not days.

Once this happened to me while I was having lunch with my mom at a spa resort. Another time, at a winery while wine-tasting with a friend in Napa Valley. I swear, the winery's bathroom was a mile away. I'm sure people were like, "Why is that lady frantically running and covering her butt. She must be drunk."

If they only knew.

It's easy for me to laugh about it now that the intense fear and anxiety have dissipated.

After almost five years of dealing with this, I had a procedure done where I went under anesthesia (best nap ever!) and my OBGYN doctor discovered that my cervix had nearly closed completely. After my doctor fixed the issue, my menstrual symptoms were significantly reduced. Thank God!

She also found new, abnormal cells that she was able to remove. As you can imagine, I'm now a huge advocate for preventative care. Because I went to my annual routine OBGYN appointment, the cancerous cells were caught extremely early, and I am blessed to still be here today.

According to the World Health Organization, in 2020, cancer was the leading cause of death at approximately 10 million deaths from cancers worldwide (nearly 1 out of every 6 deaths that year).[5] Cancer mortality rates can be significantly reduced through prevention, early detection, and treatment.

According to the American Cancer Society, the five-year survival and success rate for certain localized cancers with early detection are:

- Basal and Squamous Cell Carcinoma Skin Cancer (melanoma): 99%[6]

- Bladder Cancer (localized): 70%[7]
- Bone Cancer (not spread outside of the bone where it originated): 91%[8]
- Breast Cancer (cancer that is confined to the breast): 99%[9]
- Cervical Cancer (stage 0 or 1): 92%[10]
- Colon Cancer (not spread to nearby lymph nodes): 91%[11]
- Localized kidney cancer (stage I and II): 93%[12]
- Liver Cancer (stage 1): 36%[13]
- Lung Cancer (not spread beyond the lungs): 65%[14]
- Pancreatic Cancer (not spread beyond the pancreas): 44%[15]
- Prostate Cancer (still confined to the prostate): 100%[16]
- Thyroid Cancer (Papillary, Follicular or Medullary; excludes Anaplastic): 100%[17]

These numbers are not meant to scare you. They show that even cancer can be treatable, if caught at an early stage. Early detection is key! Allow information such as this to encourage you to stay on top of completing your preventative care on a regular basis.

The Crazy Hormone Show

Cancer has the highest risk of returning within the first five years, and it could show its ugly face anywhere in the body. I had to be on high alert during that time period. It was during the early part of these five years that I vowed to educate myself about healthy nutrition and take responsibility for my eating habits.

I couldn't control whether the cancer came back or not; the only things I had control over were staying active and eating healthy. If I stayed fit and focused on my food choices, and the cancer still came back, then I would know I'd done everything I could. There would be no doubt. No regrets. But If I wasn't proactive and the cancer returned, I knew I would have regrets.

At this point, I'd mastered the fitness part of the equation, so this point began my journey toward understanding nutrition. It took years and years before this part of my life became routine, though. There were times when I "fell off" my healthy eating practices, but I was tenacious and I never gave up.

It was here that my journey for inspiring and motivating others to become healthy budded and then started to blossom.

In the summer of 2015, I decided to compete in an NBA all-natural physique competition. I was 35 years old at the time, and the division appropriate for my age was the not-at-all intimidating "Junior Bikini Divas Master."

But I wasn't participating in this to show off my super-skinny self in a bikini, nor is a physique competition any reflection of health. It's quite the opposite. My deeply meaningful motivation for doing this competition was to show women they could do anything they set their minds to. I wanted to inspire women to go after the goals that were truly important to them. I knew that I could achieve anything I set my mind to, but I wanted to help other women come to that same realization by acting as a role model.

Many times in my life, I have heard friends say how they'd love to do this, that, or the other. Seriously, just insert your goal here. But all I really heard was a self-*dis*belief in their ability and capabilities, mixed with low self-esteem and a lack of confidence.

This became my drive to pursue an insane schedule for three solid months as I prepared. Throughout my quest, I documented my schedule and process on social media, including a strict nutrition plan, proper supplementation, and waking up at 1:30 A.M. so that I could complete my strength training workout before work (I went to a 24-hour gym), shower, go to my full-time job, go back to the gym after work to do my cardio training, go to sleep by 8:30 P.M., and then wake up five hours later to start all over again.

It struck me how selfish a process like this could be, yet at the same time, I was doing it for a selfless purpose. For three months, my social life was nonexistent; all of my energy had to be saved for training and my normal work.

The training was mentally and physically challenging. By the last four weeks before my competition, I had five strength training workouts each week and one hour of steady-state cardio every single day. And my coach had me consuming a measly 900 calories per day. He was nationally known for working with competitors on "gear" (steroids). You can get away with putting your body through extreme conditions like these when you're on steroids and your body can still achieve optimal physical appearance, but as a natural competitor, this just isn't the case.

I was putting an extreme amount of stress on my body through my workouts, only allowing myself a small window of "recovery" of about five hours of sleep each night. The insufficient nutrients I consumed were hardly enough to compensate for all the energy I was losing. Understandably, my body went into survival mode. In the end, I burned fat, but also muscle. Most importantly, my hormone levels became completely off-balance.

One thing I do want to discuss briefly is the state of health, or lack of, that physique competitors are in on the day of a show. I've heard many women mention they want to look like women on stage, but this is when we are literally at our worst: We've been training to our limits, almost starving ourselves, and, by stage time, have depleted the majority of the water in our bodies. No one walks around like that on a regular basis. This is a very short-lived, temporary situation.

The same goes for most professional fitness-brand photos you've seen from one of your idolized role models. A lot happens behind the scenes that isn't shown: training, water depletion, spray tans, hair and make-up, and Photoshop. My point is this: women need to understand this is not a picture of health or real life. This is the opposite. We should always strive to be the healthiest versions of ourselves. Period.

But, I digress.

I ended up placing third in my division at my first and only competition, which was awesome. What was not awesome was, once the competition came and went, I was living in a body I didn't recognize anymore. My hormones had completely changed.

Now, I know most readers probably haven't participated in a physique competition, but any woman can relate to hormonal shifts if: You're in your 30s, 40s, 50s or beyond; you've gone through perimenopause and/or menopause; or you've had a hysterectomy, a child, or multiple children. Changes in your hormones can make you feel like a stranger in your own body. Ever felt this way?

When hormones change, many women don't take the time to be proactive in trying to return balance to their bodies or understand their new hormones and how their body reacts to fitness (or a lack thereof) and nutrition. Fully understanding how your body functions is a key aspect in transforming your body and achieving permanent weight loss.

In my circumstance, I was able to return my hormones to healthy levels, but it took me almost a year before I felt like myself again.

First, I focused on overall proper nutrition and consuming adequate amounts of healthy fats. Then, because my coach had had me consuming only about 900 calories per day, I had to slowly Reverse-Diet my calories back to a healthy amount for my lifestyle and body metrics. Reversing dieting is a way to slowly increase your calories without gaining weight. For example, at the time, 1,700 calories per day would have been my "maintenance" calories: Enough daily calories so I wasn't gaining or losing weight.

If I had increased my calories from 900 to 1,700 overnight, I would have gained weight. Instead, after my competition, I increased my calories by 150 for the next month. So, I was consuming 1,050 calories per day. The following month, I raised my calories by another 150, so I was consuming 1,200, and so on until I hit approximately 1,700. Each time, I increased all of my macros (proteins, carbohydrates, and fats). This allowed me to increase my calories and give my body time to adapt without gaining any excess weight.

If you do the math, this took five months, but remember how I mentioned it took me about a year to feel like myself again? Although I had successfully brought my calories back up to a healthy level, it took my body another seven months to feel like I was in control emotionally and with my energy levels.

My hormone imbalances brought on by my competition experience were a direct reflection of my nutritional inadequacies, elevated stress levels, and lack of proper recovery.

Ladies, balancing your hormones (stress, thyroid, and female-specific) is possible! I know what it's like to not feel like your true self. I have been there. But, with a little effort, you can feel good again!

What an amazing feeling that was, the day I realized that I truly felt like myself again. If you are proactive, there are solutions to overcoming hormone imbalances. We will discuss these options soon.

A New Path, A Higher Purpose

In early 2016, I was doing well, and it was then that a dear friend challenged me to take my years of fitness experience and knowledge to the next level. That's when I first started training fitness clients one-on-one at a local gym.

This was my first experience working with an expertise of mine that truly brought me an immense level of joy by helping others.

Then, I started my first group fitness class called Bellies & Butts at a West Sacramento gym called Pure Form Training (PFT). It was a class for women focused on strengthening the core and legs. From there, I went on to coaching group HIIT (High Intensity Interval Training) and strength-training classes at PFT. My experience and knowledge progressed, and I became an expert in exercise biomechanics. As my experience with coaching clients deepened, so did my knowledge and love of nutrition.

In August of that year, the same friend and I founded the 90-Day TruFit Challenge. We focused on customized nutrition for each of our clients. These challenges were so successful that, after five challenges, we had helped hundreds of people all over the United States lose thousands of pounds, collectively. It was an incredibly unforgettable and rewarding opportunity!

Four years later, during a time when I was customizing meal plans for my clients, I completed Precision Nutrition's Level 1 Nutrition Certification. Immediately after that, I completed their year-long master's certification and became a Precision Nutrition Master Health Coach certified in Nutrition and Change Psychology. Here, I deepened my knowledge about the power of mindset and habit change.

Long-term, I understood that there were limits to being a Fitness Coach. I mean, how many trainers do you see working out in gyms and coaching classes into their 50s, 60s, and beyond? Not many. I knew my future career path was taking me in the direction of helping others achieve a total body transformation: mind, body, and spirit. I would use this knowledge, along with my past experiences, to better help others.

A Vibrant Life Ahead

Multiple pivotal moments in my life have altered its trajectory and contributed to the evolution of what holds deep meaning for me. The journey I have revealed to you showcases the crucial "steppingstones" that led me to where I am today.

It has been a wonderful, rewarding journey helping clients achieve their health and fitness goals. I have worked with a wide range of clients, from adolescents to clients in their seventies. And this is something I can state without a doubt:

No matter what age you are, regardless of your health history, current weight, eating habits, etc., if you truly want to transform and live a healthy, vibrant life for many years to come, *it is possible!*

Our bodies adapt to everything we do, healthy and unhealthy. It may take decades for us to put on excessive weight, but in months, we can lose it all and go from being in a near-death situation to being fit, healthy, and thriving! Once you understand how all of your cells, tissues, organs, body cavities, bones, muscles, blood, nerves, and skin work together to maintain homeostasis and support overall bodily functions, you realize that *bodies are truly a living miracle.*

That is why I set out to write this book. To help as many people as possible, no matter where you are in the world, what you eat, where you work, and how you work out. Health and healthy living are universal.

Through extensive learning and experience, I have prepared for you the essential steps to becoming a weight loss success story through unorthodox, but holistic, methods. All you need to know about getting healthy, fit, discovering and loving yourself, losing weight and keeping it off, is in this book.

Information Overload

I truly believe God is in control. He has also blessed us with minds that can discern what's healthy from unhealthy, and right from wrong. In our modern society, so much pulls our time and attention; sometimes, we are so busy that we don't take the time to think much about the choices we're making regarding food, exercise, and overall healthy living.

Our casual choices often become habits, which then become routines. Those routines are generally things we do on "autopilot" and without any significant awareness.

Breaking out of those routines and habits can be done by simply following step-by-step guidance, but there's also a caveat.

Because if it were truly that simple, why do the overwhelming majority of people who quit smoking, quit drinking, start nutrition plans, sign up for fitness regimens to lose weight, get out of debt following an aggressive budgeting plan, or undertake any other change so often end up back with the same unhealthy habits?

After all, there's no shortage of nutrition plans in the world. No shortage of fitness regimens. No shortage of information.

It is because information alone does not cause transformation. It's such a simple concept, but one which is too easily overlooked. We live in the Information Age, and our access to information has increased rapidly. Exponentially, in fact.

Simply go online from your smartphone and you can find out just about anything you want. In fact, you'll have access to tons of reliable, quality information on nearly every topic imaginable ... as well as access to *unreliable* information.

If information was all we needed, we would all be rich, happy, and fit, right? But most of us are not; we generally lack one or more of these three things. And as a society, we are most certainly not rich, happy, and thin.

In fact, our society is getting unhealthier, heavier, and facing more serious health issues than any generation before. Why?

The problem is rooted in something deeper: Meaning.

This book will allow you to truly understand what is deeply meaningful to you and then provide the guidance that will set you up for success no matter what you are striving for. Ideally, you should complete this book before you tackle any of your priorities or goals. This is what I call **Vision before Victory**.

More importantly, I will show you how self-sustaining, transformational change happens at a much deeper level.

It starts from within.

Don't worry – we'll be discussing and developing this in Part 3.

It is important to note that some people who are overweight are struggling with chronic health issues or disabilities. This can make it almost impossible for them to take all of the steps needed to improve their health. In cases like this, it's important to stick to one's personal healthcare provider's guidance before making any decisions. Any advice offered here does not take the place of a doctor's recommendations, nor should it be considered official healthcare advice for you.

Part 2

Lasting Change is Multifaceted

"There are no constraints on the human mind, no walls around the human spirit, no barriers to our progress except those we ourselves erect." — Ronald Reagan

Matters of the Mind

The human brain is arguably the most incredible thing in the universe. Human beings have the capacity to imagine things beyond our reality, to dream, and to make a conscious decision to alter the course of one's life.

The brain is often referred to as the mind. This is because it's not just about the brain and its physiological processes (neurons, synapses, and electrical impulses that make it all work), but also about our emotions, mentality, and thought processes. All these things comprise the mind.

While the distinction between "brain" and "mind" may seem inconsequential, it is critical. If we continue to think about our brain as merely another organ in the body, then its functions exist on a merely biological plane. Yet, you are not defined by the way your brain works; for most people, the brain works essentially the same as every other person's brain does.

That is why it is important to understand that your mind is more than the sum of the parts of your brain. The mind is the part of you that allows you to feel emotions, to perceive, to think, and have unique experiences with others, as well as to remember, possess personal desires, and, of course, imagine.

Author Napoleon Hill of *Think and Grow Rich*, discusses a state of mind that uses autosuggestion, also known as self-suggestion. Autosuggestion acts as a communication channel between the conscious part of the mind and the subconscious part; by sending stimuli to one's mind through our five senses.

Only through the Principle of Autosuggestion can positive or negative thoughts enter the subconscious mind. Whether driven by fear, courage, or faith, the subconscious mind manifests thoughts into one's reality.

Napoleon Hill also references the law of autosuggestion in which any individual has the potential to achieve accomplishment:

> "If you *think* you are beaten, you are.
> If you *think* you dare not, you don't.
> If you like to win, but you *think* you can't,
> it is almost certain you won't.
>
> If you *think* you'll lose, you're lost.
> For out of the world we find,
> success begins with a person's will –
> it's all in the *state of mind.*
>
> If you *think* you are outclassed, you are.
> You've got to *think* high to rise.
> You've got to be *sure of yourself* before
> you can ever win a prize.
> Life's battles don't always go
> to the stronger or faster man,

but sooner or later the one who wins
is the one WHO THINKS HE CAN!"[18]

This describes perfectly how your thoughts, and self-talk, can play a huge role in potentially altering many aspects of your life, including achieving, or not achieving, success.

If this is an area for you that has room for improvement, think about practices that you can incorporate into your daily routine to improve this. There are endless possibilities, but here are some examples: repeating a positive word mantra throughout your day, taking the time to acknowledge your daily accomplishments, engaging in tasks that give you a sense of productivity, and so on.

These conscious practices will end up positively affecting your subconscious mind.

The Levels of Logic

Consciousness refers to our subjective awareness of ourselves, our surroundings, and our experiences. It involves being awake and perceiving sensations, thoughts, and emotions, as well as having a sense of self. Consciousness allows us to perceive and interact with the world, engage in thought processes, and experience our own existence. It is a fundamental aspect of human experience and the basis for our ability to perceive, think, reason, and make decisions.

Subconsciousness, on the other hand, is the processes of the brain that operate below the level of conscious awareness. Your subconscious mind represents thoughts, feelings, desires, and memories that are not currently in the forefront of your conscious awareness, but still have influence on your behaviors, emotions, and perceptions.

The subconscious mind is believed to play a significant role in shaping one's beliefs, attitudes, habits, and automatic responses. The subconscious mind processes information and stimuli without conscious effort and can store vast amounts of information. It can also impact dreams, creativity, and problem-solving abilities.

There are many aspects to the mind that involve consciousness and subconsciousness. Every time you face a new situation and must adapt, part of that is done on the conscious level while another part occurs on the subconscious level.

Let's summarize: Your mind is the product of your brain, mental attitude, mental processes, opinions, intelligence, behaviors, and emotions. Your emotions are a state of feeling, and the affective aspect of consciousness is typically accompanied by physiological and behavioral changes in the body.

When you begin to understand and accept that long-lasting change is multifaceted and that it comprises the mind, body, and spirit, you can then begin to address all of these areas to help promote success.

The mind is the most important of these.

Long-lasting change cannot start with the body. With no mental preparation, your body wouldn't know what to do. For example, if you haven't thought about what your goals are and how you plan to accomplish them, how would your body know what to do once you're ready to start working out? Same goes for fueling your body with the proper nutrition. If you haven't decided what foods align with your goals or support your fitness regimen, how will you know what to buy and how fuel your body appropriately?

Long-lasting change does not start with your spirit. This is a system of values guiding the soul or the discerning mind, which, in turn, makes judgments or choices. Our minds take the experiences we've had and shapes our values, morals, standards, and boundaries. For example, it would be challenging to acknowledge our values and morals if we haven't first engaged in cognitive reflection on our experiences, encompassing both nurture and nature. Through self-reflection and analysis we define what is acceptable and unacceptable for the way we want to live our lives.

Mindful Motives

When I talk about mind, body, and spirit, the mind comes first.

Think about this for a moment.

If you decide one day that you are determined to run a marathon in a year, where does your training process begin? Ideally, you have a conscious plan, which starts in the mind.

For some people, ideas like randomly deciding to participate in a marathon can begin from emotions (for example, they are tired of feeling lazy or bad about their bodies) or their mental attitude (they know that jogging is a great form of exercise, helps burn calories, and increases cardiovascular strength).

If you've simply stepped out of your house with no plan or idea where you're headed, you're likely to have no real motivation to keep going (unless you're Forrest Gump). Unfortunately, this is where so many nutrition plans and exercise regimens fail.

The average person is reacting with their body.

Think of it like this: You are hungry. You might have skipped a couple of meals and it's the end of a long and difficult day. On your way to your car, you see an advertisement for a delicious-looking meal – one that is cooked to perfection. What happens? Your body reacts to the stimuli (because of your mind). Your body craves the end result. Maybe you swing into that restaurant and order what you saw on the billboard. And let's say this will set you back a little in your healthy nutrition plan and fitness goals, at least as far as the calories are concerned.

What happens then? You might feel guilty. Regret may cling to you. That's your mind doing its thing. However, this process is unfolding in the opposite manner from what is needed to create long-lasting change. In this example, the process first started in the body and then went to the mind second.

I want you to hold onto the notion that everything we are discussing here relates back to the goal of long-lasting change. If change does not begin in the mind, then permanent change is less likely to happen.

In your mind, you have conscious thoughts, subconscious processes, actions and reactions, and emotions. All of these work together splendidly to begin building a bridge to lasting change.

Meet Allison

Allison was a mother of two in her forties who had overcome numerous challenges in the past, including addiction. She was a buoyant, energized woman who was emotionally charged.

Before I met her, Allison had already overcome an addiction. As with many people who deal with addiction, hers was not an over-and-done-with recovery, but rather a series of successes and losses, ups and downs, trials and errors, until she finally managed to get beyond the chains that had bound her to those "demons."

Someone who can overcome any real addiction – whether it is drugs, alcohol, sex, or any number of other vices that grab people during times of weakness – is a person with fortitude.

Allison most certainly had determination. There were several unhealthy habits in her life that she'd managed to overcome, so I had no doubt she would be able to put that same fortitude and determination into working towards her health goals.

Yet, Allison admitted to me that she was constantly falling into unhealthy habits when it came to exercise and nutrition.

Remember when I said that the mind is a composite of many things, including subconscious actions? This is where many unhealthy habits can lie. These kinds of habits are something we do without considering them. They may have started as a reaction to some stimuli, but continued time and time again, and eventually you begin doing them without having to consciously think about them at all.

That was part of the challenge for Allison, especially in relation to exercise and nutrition. She was constantly finding herself slipping back into old habits.

When you are dealing with addiction recovery, unhealthy eating and sedentary habits can often become comfortable fallbacks. These vices develop as a means to replace the other addiction. A person wants to overcome an addiction, so sometimes they turn to something else to distract themselves from the desires their body has (physically or physiologically). In time, those other behaviors can become habits, maybe even other addictions.

Eating can be an addiction. So can having a sedentary lifestyle. If you're spending most of your time watching TV or sitting down, you'll eventually have less desire to do physical activity. Your body will always try to be as comfortable as possible. It is a survival instinct. Some of these behaviors aren't technically classified as addictions, but a person can truly become addicted to nearly anything, be it sugar, caffeine, gambling, exercise, etc.

With Allison, I understood immediately that she had the tools to overcome addiction and challenges. She had done it already. I had no doubt about her capabilities.

What I immediately determined was that this was likely a matter of priorities. Or ... a lack of priorities.

This was a cognitive concern that needs to be addressed, but not just for Allison. It needs to be addressed by all of us who wish to change some aspects of our lives and yet find that we keep procrastinating from putting forth the effort. I could have given Allison an exercise program and a meal plan of what foods to eat and what to try avoiding, but would that have been enough?

No, not for Allison. As I mentioned, she had the tools to overcome addiction, but she admitted she kept "falling short" when she started working towards new health goals.

If it had been a matter of information and her ability to follow through, then these plans and routines would have sufficed.

For Allison, there was conflict. Her mental and emotional states conflicted with one another. Her mind was not aligned properly for sustainable change.

Some days, she would feel positive, energetic, hopeful, and determined. She would consume all of her protein, eat her vegetables, watch her carbohydrate choices, and so on with each meal. Her emotions were aligned with fitness and nutrition. She felt motivated and inspired on these days.

Then there were times when she would feel melancholy, removed, and less confident; when that happened, she would abandon the activities that could have led to healthy living. Why? Her emotional state was directly impacting her mental state.

It's a lot easier to have your mental frame of mind go along with your plans when things are good, and you're hopeful and determined. But things don't always happen the way we expect them to, right?

Mentally, Allison knew that exercising was good for her. She knew it gave her more energy and that watching her food choices, avoiding junk food, and focusing more on wholesome meals were all good for her body and energy levels.

Emotionally, though, she desired comfort snacks (like most of us) and the opportunity to curl up on the couch and zone out on social media or by allowing TV to wash over her and help her forget the emotions she was experiencing in the moment.

Allison is just like you or me in that respect. One day, we can feel like we are on top of the world, that nothing can drag us down. Sometimes, amazing days can truly make you feel invincible!

The next day, we may wake up cheery and energized, but suddenly things don't go as planned. You drop your blazing cup of coffee and splash scalding water on your legs, or traffic doesn't budge and you're late for work. Then, later on, your kids have no idea why they are screaming and fighting, but they're hell-bent on making sure the world can hear them.

How quickly we can shift from high to low and in between! It's quite amazing, isn't it?

Allison was strong enough to overcome some serious addictions, but prior to meeting me, she found it almost impossible to manage the highs and lows life threw her way. She would undulate between feeling great, staying active, and eating healthy (or what she thought was healthy at that time) to feeling horrible and remaining sedentary, withdrawing and eating the way she felt.

I've done that. Have you? You feel miserable, heartbroken, angry, or maybe even bored. So, what do you do? Grab a pint of ice cream? Chocolate? Or those crunchy, salty chips in the pantry? It's your secret food craving that only seems to be on your mind when you're feeling a certain way, right?

Don't worry. It happens to the best of us. *You are definitely not alone.* There are many reasons a person's action steps become compromised. It could be due to boredom, exhaustion, emotional highs or lows, laziness, not having enough time, being too hungry to bother to care in that moment, frustration, stress ... and the list goes on and on!

Allison was very aware that her emotions were dictating her actions. I got her set up on an exercise routine and nutrition plan, but I also knew we had to focus on her mindset. We needed to spend valuable time processing her emotions.

I encouraged her to reflect on everything that was going on in her daily routine. I wanted to dig into what her mental, emotional, and physiological responses were to everything we were focusing on together. We needed to understand how different events during her day could be impacting her emotions, mental focus, and attitude, and see what kind of physiological responses occurred due to different stimuli in her routine.

As Allison focused on self-awareness every day, she was better able to stay on track and remain more goal-oriented. This also allowed the two of us, along with her friends and family who supported her, to celebrate the progress she made.

Why do you think we congratulate young children when they accomplish seemingly small or insignificant things? Because it reinforces the behaviors we want to see repeated from them.

Adults are no different. We love positive affirmations. Sometimes, we crave them, and yet, how often do we really get to hear that reassurance we so need?

From others? Rarely.

From ourselves? Even less often.

Celebrating progress and small victories is a critical part of maintaining a positive emotional outlook on the changes we're pursuing in life.

Honoring progress and successes, no matter how minor they may seem, can be a powerful way to elevate self-love. Choosing to not love yourself, will open the door to negative thoughts that can create unwanted conflicts between your mental and emotional mindsets.

Self-love is powerful, and with small victories and the celebrations, Allison developed a heightened sense of self-love. This positive reinforcement for her new, healthy habits and behaviors encouraged her to keep working toward her goals.

As we worked together, Allison was able to objectively make better decisions without the input of any irrational emotions, and this helped her stay focused and reach her goals.

Takeaways from Allison

Allison had a host of unhealthy habits that swirled around throughout her life. The more she came to understand those thoughts and emotions, what triggered them and how to recognize them for what they were, the better she was able to stand her ground when they tried to creep back into her life.

Eliminating emotional and mental lows from your life is impossible. Things happen whether you want them to or not. We have rough stretches. We experience hard events. But, by creating awareness and understanding how you are reacting to these things, you can learn to positively change your future reactions.

Additionally, some of us may still be holding onto regrets or mistakes from our past. To find self-love, confidence, and belief in oneself, we must be capable of forgiving ourselves and letting go to move forward.

It took many years before I had that *Aha* moment of self-awareness for myself. In my 20s, I didn't have control over my temper. First off, I would get frustrated with inanimate objects. Have you ever dropped or spilled something? I mean, it happens to all of us. But in my 20s, things like that frustrated me so much.

And have you ever gotten mad at other drivers? I think most people have at least once in their life. I used to have so many pet peeves about other drivers, it sometimes turned into road rage.

At some point, thankfully, I realized my frustration was pointless. I was only upsetting myself, negatively affecting my day; I decided I didn't want to be that angry person I sometimes was behind the wheel.

Often times, the only way we can learn to correct our behavior is by experiencing situations similar to those which have set off the behavior before, but then making a conscious decision to react differently. At first, the reactions will still be "kneejerk" reactions. If your goal to change something in your life is truly important to you, though, you will work diligently on it over time. Eventually, you will be slower to react in that kneejerk fashion and will choose different, more positive ways to respond going forward.

This is the journey I took. One day, I realized the way I was reacting to things was not in line with the person I aspired to be.

After making the decision to invest effort in changing the way I responded to frustrating situations, I spent many years simply building awareness of these situations.

Initially, the reactions remain consistent because my mind processed the situation more slowly than my immediate responses.

In the initial phase of the corrective process, I continued to experience feelings of regret or guilt for my initial reactions, yet my determination to change remained unwavering.

The more opportunities that arise to respond in a more positive manner, the more I came to realize that it's all about staying present and making conscious decisions about everything happening throughout my daily life.

Let's be candid here. It's also about letting go of your ego. Your ego can be your adversary. When your reactions are fueled by your ego, it becomes all about you. For instance, *how dare that person use the gym equipment I want, or how dare that person merge into my lane while I'm driving.* Your ego can be rather narcissistic, standing in stark contrast to showing courtesy, compassion, and respect to others, no matter how they treat you.

If you're interested in diving deeper into the human ego, I highly recommend *A New Earth* by Eckhart Tolle. It's one of my all-time favorite reads and has the potential to be life-changing.

It's not just about the ego. For some of us, our negative reactions to frustrating situations can stem from subconsciously realizing that we lack control over the circumstances. To release our grip on the "control wheel," we must find peace in acknowledging that we can't control everything, such as the weather, how others drive, the emotions, actions, or words of others, and so forth. However, we always have control over our actions and how we choose to react. When faced with something beyond your control, it's essential to let it go.

Allow your ego to do the same.

Otherwise, you may end up carrying those negative emotions with you for years, or, even worse, indefinitely.

By making a conscious effort to let go of the things I could not control, checking my ego, and being present with my emotional reactions, I was able to slowly start to make progress to positively modify my behaviors.

Progress is never always going forward. When we're making progress, we go forward, fall back, move forward again, and then fall back again.

In my case, having control over my emotional reactions was deeply meaningful to me. I did not want my temper to control me, so I took control. For me, it took decades before I finally realized that I had conquered and gained control of my emotions. I am a much more "Zen" person now. The 20-something-year-old version of me would be extremely proud.

Let's reflect on how we emotionally respond to things when we're challenged, frustrated, disappointed, etc. These reactions could come from our environment growing up, past relationships, something we were taught in school, what our friends did, or something picked up from any other source. Maybe an emotional reaction to a challenging day typically has you trolling the cupboards for a late night snack. You're most likely not hungry but have created a habit that's become routine and now just feels good. To understand why this is happening, we have to find the trigger is.

Become aware of any possible triggers that happen around you or to you, which create emotional reactions. Triggers are subconscious responses to certain stimuli that set off emotional reactions. These can stem from a memory of a positive or negative experience. For example, maybe, while growing up, your parents told you that you had to eat everything on your dinner plate. If you didn't, you had to eat it for breakfast. Over time, this could have created an irrational eating habit and a negative emotional response to dinnertime. The origin of this emotional response and behavior stemmed from the experience with your parents. The trigger is any situation you are not hungry or full, and you still have food on your plate. You'll then feel the need to finish what's left on your plate. Even worse are the psychological responses to your actions once you do finish your dinner: feeling ashamed, upset, bad about yourself, and so on.

It's important to remember that both emotional reactions and triggers are things you can work on through awareness and intention. We are trying to shift the balance from subconscious thought processes and behaviors to conscious awareness and an ability to stand your ground during times of temptation.

Self-reflection is the key.

Below are some questions I had Allison begin asking herself when she became aware that she was reacting emotionally to things. These questions brought her to a heightened *awareness* of the mindset triggers that encourage unhealthy habits. Additionally, I included an example. You can use these, too, when you begin striving for long-lasting healthy changes in your life.

- *What am I thinking about?* For example, let's say you've stopped in at the local café for a latte before work. You already had a smoothie or a couple of eggs and some berries for breakfast, but right there in the café's glass case is a mouthwatering cookie that seems to be staring at you.

- *What are my emotions and desires?* You probably feel like you're being hypnotized by that cookie and start rationalizing why you think you deserve it. This is a very common reaction. When we get something we want, our brain releases dopamine, the "feel-good" neurotransmitter. We remember this feeling later, and when we're faced with the same stimuli (such as the possibility of a cookie), we want that thing again in order to feel good again.

- *Why am I thinking and feeling this way?* The answer to this question could be many things. Maybe your parents used a cookie as a reward for good behavior or a job well done when you were a child. Perhaps you were never allowed to have sweets growing up. Maybe you see that cookie, and the small rebel within you starts calling out, "I deserve that cookie!"
  Only you know the answer to this question, and it's important to be honest with yourself. You're not going to win any points by lying to yourself, your mentor, family member, friend, therapist, or anyone else who's helping you along this journey. Remember, these questions are for you. You don't have to share the answers with anyone if you don't want to.

- *When do these thoughts and emotions tend to be strongest?* One of the first critical aspects of self-awareness is analyzing when various thoughts and emotions begin to stir within you. For example, a person who craves a delicious-looking cookie may only have cravings for this while walking past a bakery display. Other people may notice the cookie aisle at their local grocery store and feel unable to avoid it. Still others may have specific thoughts and emotions late at night, or at the end of a long day when they're craving something sweet to help them forget their stress levels. It's important to begin recognizing when certain emotions begin getting triggered within you because there is almost always a pattern. Allison figured out what was triggering certain emotions in her, and that level of self-awareness helped empower her. How? When you notice certain thoughts or emotions developing in specific circumstances or following certain stimuli, you can figure out a way to avoid those stimuli, at least until you know they no longer control you.

Remember, when you are seeking lasting, effective change in your life, the challenges are going to be real and tremendous. Just because you may have to avoid the local bakery or your favorite coffee shop that has the delicious cinnamon buns on display for the next few weeks (or months), it doesn't mean it's always going to be that way.

This is about figuring out what the unhealthy triggers are that shape your emotional responses. Here are a couple of questions to help you better *understand* your triggers and help you refocus:

- *Is this going to help me reach my goals or move me further away from them?* The answer to this question is going to be a simple yes or no. There really is no in-between. If thoughts or emotions are driving you back to old self-sabotaging habits, then understanding where they come from is going to help you reach your goals. Your self-awareness will empower you to do what is necessary to avoid those thoughts and emotions in the first place.

- *How can I learn from these unhealthy triggers to make a better decision next time?* If you don't know what's triggering your thoughts and emotions, you will continually find yourself in the destructive patterns that have been shaping your life. We need to fully understand the situation in front of us, especially as it pertains to our thoughts, emotions, and how they may be stimulated at different times.

For example, to help you *learn* from these thoughts and emotions, ask yourself a few pointed questions:

- *When is my willpower at its lowest?* Most of us don't think much about our willpower until we start analyzing difficult situations more closely. For some, your willpower might disappear during social events or when at a restaurant. For others, it might be staying home alone at night that triggers a craving for a late-night snack which the body doesn't need.
  If you can pinpoint when your willpower is lowest, you become empowered through knowledge. That empowerment breeds confidence and increases your capacity to take control of those situations and circumstances, just as Allison was able to do.

- *What is making self-control difficult?* For example, you may be at a social gathering and your friends are drinking. You want to fit in, or at least partake with everyone else, so you enjoy your favorite adult beverage. If you already have issues with drinking too much, or simply lack self-control, that seemingly innocent drink can quickly turn into two, three, or potentially more.
  Or maybe you're at a nice restaurant enjoying a healthy entrée. You might feel proud of yourself about your healthy choices. Then, you spot a luscious dessert on a table nearby, and it looks de-licious!
  Or you're at home, and the stress of the day has worn you down. In the past, having a snack brought comfort, and you know this is

something no one will know about. It's just a little secret between you and yourself. Besides, what harm can a single, insignificant snack pose? Of course, many of us already know the answer to this question.

- *Where am I when this is happening?* Are you at a party or out to dinner? Are you by yourself at home, at work, driving, or somewhere else? The *what* and the *where* typically go hand in hand. Again, take note of this.

- *Why has my willpower been compromised?* Often, I notice clients express that their willpower is weakest after they've had a bad day at work. It doesn't matter what type of job you have, whether you work one full-time job or several part-time jobs, whether you are an executive, nurse, real estate agent, or stay-at-home mom; everyone has bad days at work at some point. A bad day at work can trigger those negative emotions that lead you to make poor decisions about your health and nutrition.
  Maybe you've argued with your spouse, a friend, or a co-worker. Maybe you're stressed, have health issues, or are worried about your finances. All of these things can contribute to restless nights. For many people, a lack of sleep can leaves them feeling emotionally drained, fatigued, and vulnerable. When you're exhausted, your willpower will feel almost nonexistent.

- *How can I set myself up for success next time?* You set yourself up for success by knowing what triggers certain thoughts and emotions which lead to poor decisions. Also, understanding your vision, mission, and goals will help you create a "plan of attack" for the next time you're confronted with similar difficult situations.

Do not think of those situations as circumstances, but rather as *triggers* or *stimuli.* If you keep those two words in the front of your mind, it will help you find better focus and remove all emotional attachment, allowing you to reflect objectively.

Also, I want you to understand – and this is very important – *you are not alone in this struggle.* I have faced this time and time again in my life. Everyone around you, every single person you know or will meet in your lifetime, has or is dealing with very similar challenges.

Your struggles might be different than the next person's, but that doesn't make theirs any less or greater than yours. It's important not to get down on yourself or feel like you're a "failure" simply because a yummy cookie triggers a desire deep within you that leads you down the wrong path.

Every single one of us faces desires, whatever they may be, every single day. Building self-awareness and understanding what your unhealthy triggers may be are the first steps in developing and knowing what your plan of attack will be the next time around.

For example, let's say a lack of sleep causes you to wake up in a negative mindset. You know exhaustion can be a trigger for you. What can you do to set your mood back on the right path after a rough night? Get some time to yourself? Meditate for a few minutes? Drive a different, more scenic route to work? Leave a few minutes earlier to give yourself time to listen to an extra motivational song or podcast?

Perhaps the stimulus is having a bad day at work. If this is the case, and the bakery with those darn cookies is on your route home, have a game plan to take a different way home.

If you're not aware of your unhealthy triggers, you will never be able to have a game plan to avoid the temptation that so easily entangles every single one of us.

What I recommended for Allison, and what I recommend for you, was that she keep a journal to take note of every single situation she found herself in where unhealthy habits recurred. This could be a physical journal, a note pad app, or a text or audio file you send yourself, etc.

This process can feel a bit odd at first, or difficult to remember to do, but understand this: It's easy to dismiss things when they're only in your mind. You can convince yourself that the situation you *thought* was a trigger wasn't nearly as bad as it felt (at the time).

But if you write everything down, carefully documenting each situation, you will begin to see patterns. There will be no way for you to convince yourself it didn't happen or wasn't quite the way you remember. This gives you more power over these unhealthy triggers and stimuli while also helping you better understand how to be more prepared the next time they happen.

Trust me, it's not a matter of *if* they happen again, but when. If we keep that in mind, we can better control our state of mind, which, as you will recall, includes your mental attitude as well as your emotions. Every thought and action then becomes conscious.

You can wrestle the power of your life from subconscious to conscious decisions that you can then control each and every moment of the day.

Self-Discovery: Your Mental + Emotional Health

Here is a simple exercise.

You may use a blank sheet of paper or use the provided free workbook download available on my website (link at the beginning of this book.).

First, list all of the thoughts and emotions that have been consuming your mind recently (outside of reading this book).

And remember, it's very important that these exercises are done openly and honestly. No one is grading you here. No one will judge you. This is all *for you* and creating awareness.

Second, write down *why* you are having these thoughts and emotions. It could be as obvious as grief from the loss of a family member. It might be financial stress. It could also be something less obvious, something you will have to dig a little bit more for. However long it takes you to figure out the *why*, give yourself that time. Don't rush through this part.

Also, you may note what those emotions are, but the realization of why you are experiencing them may not come to you right now. That's okay. Allow the awareness of these emotions to "bounce around" in your head until you start to understand where they stem from. We often think we know why we're feeling a certain way, but the superficial reason isn't truly the answer. We need to "peel away the layers" to find the true, deeper meaning.

On a side note, one exercise I like to do with clients is to ask them *why* they think they're experiencing certain emotions. (This also helps us understand why we engage in any self-sabotaging habits.) Once they've given an answer, I'll ask, "Why?" again. This is typically asked a minimum of five times until we finally uncover the *true* reason for their emotions. I'm sure this reminds you of a toddler who tenaciously asks their parent, "Why? But, why?" Unbeknownst to us, these toddlers are little geniuses trying to uncover the truth.

Third, for each of these thoughts and emotions you wrote down, once you've found out why they're occurring in your life right now, figure out if they're helping or hindering your personal growth. Not every thought or emotion is a hindrance to the goals we have. Sometimes, they can be beneficial, motivational, or uplifting.

If this part of the exercise seems a little odd, go back to the first step of listing all of your current thoughts and emotions, and make sure you've not just focused on the negative or unhealthy ones. This is something I've noticed with clients throughout the years. After discussing all these triggers and stimuli, when tasked with writing down and figuring out the thoughts and emotions they're experiencing, most people tend to focus on the negative ones. Yet, there might be plenty of *positive* thoughts, feelings, and emotions they're feeling at that very moment.

Positive thoughts and emotions can be great inspirations to help drive us to succeed. But negative emotions can also motivate and help us cultivate personal growth. That's why this step is to figure out if your thoughts and emotions are helping or hindering your personal growth.

For those that are hindering growth, write down the thoughts and emotions you would like to improve. Sure, it's easy to say, "All of them," but that's not generally the case. There are going to be a few that really interfere with what you aim to achieve in your life. Those are the ones you will want to focus on improving first.

Fourth, are any current obstacles in your life interfering with your ability to address these thoughts and emotions?

It is vitally important that we understand our undesirable thoughts and emotions so that we can remove them from our lives and make room for the ones that are genuinely fulfilling. This book will show you how to do that.

The Power of the Body

"To keep the body in good health is a duty. Otherwise, we shall not be able to keep our mind strong and clear." — Buddha

Internally, the physical body is the arrangement of particles. It is the structure or substance of a person's material makeup. Within each of our bodies are systems within systems. It's mind-blowing to me how many systems automatically operate within my body all the time. For example, you have your cardiovascular system, which includes your heart, arteries, veins, and white and red blood cells, just to name a few. Within the heart are four chambers and valves moving blood cells through each chamber to remove carbon dioxide and then fill them with oxygen to be carried on to other cells throughout the body. Those white blood cells fight infections, viruses, bacteria, and germs.

We are complex organisms, self-contained living systems composed of organs, tissue, cells, and extracellular material. In order for every cell in our body to work at optimal efficiency, it needs the proper nutrition.

Our autonomic nervous system (ANS) is responsible for regulating various involuntary bodily functions. It consists of two branches: the sympathetic nervous system (SNS) and the parasympathetic nervous system (PSNS). Let's briefly discuss the autonomic nervous system because it's important to understanding how our body responds when we react to situations. Our body perceives experiences as stressful or restful. Striving to remove ourselves from as many stressful circumstances as possible helps us manage stress and increases our body's ability to lose weight and get fit with less effort.

The sympathetic nervous system (SNS) controls several physiological responses that prepare the body for action and help us deal with stressful or threatening situations. It is often associated with the "fight-or-flight" response, which prepares the body for action. The SNS influences:

- *Increased Heart Rate*: The SNS stimulates the heart to beat faster, increasing blood flow and oxygen delivery to muscles and organs.
- *Dilated Pupils*: The SNS causes eye pupils to dilate, allowing more light to enter and improving visual sensitivity.
- *Bronchodilation*: The SNS relaxes the smooth muscles in one's airways, resulting in the dilation of bronchioles and increased airflow to the lungs.
- *Decreased Salivation*: The SNS reduces salivary gland secretion, slowing the digestion of food.
- *Inhibited Digestion*: The SNS slows down or temporarily inhibits digestive processes, decreasing stomach activity and inhibiting peristalsis (intestinal contractions).
- *Increased Blood Pressure*: The SNS constricts blood vessels, leading to increased blood pressure and directing blood flow to vital organs and muscles.
- *Enhanced Glucose Release*: The SNS stimulates the liver to release glucose into the bloodstream, providing additional energy for the body during times of stress.
- *Adrenaline Release*: The SNS triggers the release of adrenaline (epinephrine) from adrenal glands, which further enhances physiological responses to stress.[19,20,21]

The parasympathetic nervous system (PSNS) controls several physiological functions that promote relaxation, rest, and digestion. It is often referred to as the "rest and digest" response and maintains the body's internal environment. The PSNS controls:

- *Slowed Heart Rate*: The PSNS decreases the heart rate and helps regulate blood pressure, promoting a state of relaxation.
- *Constricted Pupils*: The PSNS constricts eye pupils, reducing the amount of incoming light and improving focus on close-up objects.
- *Increased Salivation*: The PSNS stimulates salivary gland secretion, aiding in the digestion of food.
- *Enhanced Digestion*: The PSNS promotes digestion by increasing gastrointestinal activity, stimulating the release of digestive enzymes, and allows your pancreas to make and release insulin, helping your body break down sugars into cells you can use and enhancing nutrient absorption.
- *Constricted Airways*: The PSNS tightens airway muscles to constrict, which ultimately reduces the amount of work your lungs do during times of rest.
- *Stimulated Urination*: The PSNS increases bladder contraction and relaxes the urinary sphincter, facilitating and controlling urination and defecation.
- *Sexual Arousal*: The PSNS plays a role in sexual arousal and function by promoting increased blood flow to the genital area.[21,22,23]

The parasympathetic nervous system (PSNS) works in opposition to the sympathetic nervous system (SNS) to maintain balance and homeostasis in the body. The coordinated activity of both systems helps regulate various bodily functions and adapt to changing environmental demands. This chart simplifies the SNS and PSNS:

	Sympathetic Nervous System (SNS)	Parasympathetic Nervous System (PSNS)
Originates in	Originates in the thoracic and lumbar regions of the spinal cord	Originates in the sacral region of the spinal cord and the medulla
Key function	Controls body's response to perceived threats	Regulates the body's functions at rest
State activated	Fight or flight	Rest and digest
Effect on adrenaline	Yes	No
Effect on heart rate	Increases heart rate	Decreases heart rate
Effect on lungs	Bronchial tubes dilate	Bronchial tubes contract
Effect on muscles	Muscles contract	Muscles relax
Effect on pupils	Pupils dilate	Pupils constrict
Effect on digestive system	Digestive function decreases	Digestive function increases
Effect on saliva production	Saliva production decreases	Saliva production increases
Effect on mucus production	Mucus production decreases	Mucus production increases
Effect on urine secretion	Urine secretion decreases	Urine secretion increases
Effect on glycogen to glucose conversion	Increased conversion of glycogen to glucose	No

Source: Biologydictionary.net, 2021.[21]

It is important to understand how vital proper nutrition and exercise are to feeling amazing, full of energy, and balanced. We live in a society that's overwhelmed by multimillion-dollar marketing campaigns for fast food, quick meals, fad diets, sugary beverages, and all sorts of unhealthy food items and habits. Every day, the average consumer is exposed to an incredible number of advertisements. Each of us may pay limited attention to most of them and only remember a few obvious ones.

According to many digital marketing experts, most Americans are exposed to around 4,000 to 10,000 ads each day. Advertising Row reports, "The average modern person is exposed to around 5,000 ads per day."[24] In May of 2023, Statista reported about how "the United States remains indisputably the largest advertising market in the world," with the "forecast that the U.S. ad industry revenue will grow by 2.6 percent in 2023, reaching a record-high of 352 billion U.S. dollars."[25] Worldwide, ad media owners' revenue will "grow by about six percent to a record-high of 856 billion U.S. dollars."[26] An obscene amount of money is being poured into advertising each year. It's absolutely mind-blowing.

Pay attention for the next day or two. When you go online, check your email; notice the sheer volume of ads in your junk folder and the ones that somehow make it into your inbox. That's just the start. On your cell phone, if you play games or use apps, you'll see ads. If you go to websites, you'll likely see more ads. Drive to work or take public transportation, and you'll see ads on billboards, on the sides of buildings, and in the windows of stores you drive by. They're airing during every television program and in the middle of YouTube videos, all social media platforms, and also product placement.

Many of those ads have one thing in common: finding a way to help you feel good in a particular moment. A fast-food chain will hire marketing experts to make their key menu items look savory and delicious, in order to elicit a physical and emotional response in each of us. When you're hungry or in a moment of weakness, you'll see that ad and remember what the product tastes like, or imagine what it could taste like, and your body says, "Yes!"

As I noted in the previous section, one little snack might not seem like a big deal, but it's the pattern that develops as a result that has impact. We give in to those marketing campaigns when we drive up to our favorite fast-food restaurant and devour a burger and fries with a soft drink (or milkshake). In the moment, we think, "It's just once. It doesn't matter." But then we end up repeating the action and create an unhealthy pattern.

What kind of nutrition did your body just receive after such a fast-food snack? Not much. And that's the big problem. Nutrition is the energy source for our body. What we eat determines the type of energy, and how much energy, we'll have for the rest of the day.

Have you ever noticed that when you're hungry and have something with little to no real nutritional value, even though you may be full and feel satisfied immediately after devouring it, an hour or two later, your stomach feels completely empty; even worse, your body feels drained. You feel as though you're ready to take a nap.

There's an immediate and intimate connection between the physical body and the nutrition it takes in. Think of your body as a high-performance sports car. If you don't take care of that vehicle and put in the high-octane fuel it requires, or if you don't change the oil regularly, what's going to happen?

That car is going to begin to sputter. Fuel efficiency will decline, or your engine oil will turn gritty and black as tar. It will run rough, might struggle to start on cold mornings, and ultimately have a lower life expectancy overall.

It's the same for us. If we neglect our bodies by depriving them of the nutrients they need, we're going to feel the consequences of that. We're going to feel it in our joints, diminished strength, low motivation, low energy, and so on.

Ultimately, we get our energy from food, and we expend that energy to move and stay alive. This fundamental biochemical relationship between energy in (food) and energy out (metabolism and movement) is also called our energy balance.

ENERGY BALANCE

FACTORS THAT INFLUENCE 'ENERGY IN'

APPETITE
Influenced by hormones that regulate appetite and satiety

FOOD CONSUMED
Influenced by availability, palatability, energy density, sleep quality, education, socioeconomic status, and culture

CALORIES ABSORBED
Influenced by macronutrient intake, food prep, age, personal microbiome, health status, and energy status

PSYCHOLOGICAL FACTORS
Influenced by stress levels, mindset, perceived control, self-esteem, and sleep quality

FACTORS THAT INFLUENCE 'ENERGY OUT'

ENERGY BURNED AT REST
Influenced by body size, hormonal status, dieting history, genetic factors, health status, sleep quality, and age

ENERGY BURNED THROUGH EXERCISE
Influenced by exercise ability, intensity, duration, frequency, type, environment, hormonal status, and sleep quality

ENERGY BURNED BY NON-EXERCISE ACTIVITY
Influenced by health status, energy status, stress levels, hormonal status, occupation, leisure activities, and genetic factors

ENERGY BURNED BY METABOLIZING FOOD
Influenced by macronutrient makeup and how processed the food is

This isn't a comprehensive list of factors, but rather a snapshot of the most common ones. It's important to know that elements on both sides of the scale are influenced by: each other, hormones (e.g. leptin, thyroid), sleep, stress, medical conditions, pharmaceuticals, and more. This means none of these things invalidate CICO. Rather, they influence how many calories we absorb and how many we burn. And this is what leads to weight gain or loss.

For more info: precisionnutrition.com

Adapted from Alan Aragon's CICO scale, alanaragon.com

Precision Nutrition[27]

What happens when we *don't* practice good nutrition and dietary habits? We leave ourselves exposed to those bacteria, germs, viruses, and even cancers which can start developing internally and take hold of our bodies.

Some have said that "cancer feeds off sugar." While scientific studies show this link to be inconsistent, sugar can indirectly contribute to the development of cancer. Excessive sugar intake is a key risk factor of obesity, type 2 diabetes, and cardiovascular diseases. *The American Journal of Clinical Nutrition* did a study on the associations of total and added sugar consumption and cancer risk specific to overall cancer, and breast and prostate cancer, specifically. It took into consideration sugar types and their sources.

They found that *total* sugar intake was associated with higher overall cancer risk, especially when it came to breast cancer. Additionally, significant associations with risk of cancer occurred with *added* sugar intake, such as: free sugars, sucrose, sugars from milk-based desserts, dairy products, and sugary drinks.[28]

The American Heart Association recommends limiting your daily added sugar intake[29] to:

- *Women*: 6 teaspoons (25 grams or 100 calories)
- *Men*: 9 teaspoons (36 grams or 150 calories)

In general, if your body isn't getting the right vitamins and minerals, its cellular function is going to decline. Its function will be limited, just like a sports car trying to perform with dirty oil, a clogged air filter, or low octane fuel. That's not how it was designed to run.

Nutrition involves the scientific process of nourishing the body. Proper nutrition influences a person's health in a positive way. Improper nutrition, or a lack of nutrition, is going to influence a person's health in a negative way. This all comes back to the scientific process by which a living organism utilizes food, whether for growth or replacing tissue in the body.

There was a documentary quite a few years ago called *Super-Size Me*. In this documentary, Morgan Spurlock set out to determine how healthy or unhealthy McDonald's food really was. He ate nothing but McDonald's meals for breakfast, lunch, and dinner for a 30-day period, and the stipulation was that if the cashier asked if he wanted to supersize his order, he would have to do it every time.

While the documentary has been attacked by certain companies and organizations, it brought to light some very real and serious implications, not the least of which is just how unhealthy consuming fast food every day is. By the latter half of the first month on this plan, Morgan's doctor begged him to stop. He had gained so much weight that his heart rate was at dangerous levels and his blood pressure was increasing – and this was a gentleman who had been fit and relatively healthy when he'd started.

His body was deprived of adequate nutrition, but more than that, he was pumping into his body so much processed sugar, carbohydrates, and other additives through the super-sized fries, sodas, and meals, the plan was directly and significantly affecting his health.

Now, I don't believe most people are eating fast food for breakfast, lunch, and dinner every day. This is an extreme, but documented, scenario of the effects.

The point here is that information, and awareness, are not what's lacking. We have plenty of information when it comes to nutrition, but information doesn't cause transformation.

What is Healthy Nutrition?

Good nutrition is science-based. That scientific foundation is rooted in strong research data, not simply a belief system. It's easy for people to say they think a certain food item is healthy, but you want to follow quantifiable data – research that shows why something is actually good for our body.

Consuming good nutrition enables us to better control our energy balance. Grabbing that trendy, sugary "coffee" milkshake from your favorite coffee shop, or a quick Yoplait yogurt and granola bar for lunch (because you don't have time to prepare something healthy), probably isn't giving your body the nutrition it needs. Most people think these food items are healthy and might be shocked to learn the truth.

When we focus on positive, healthy nutrition, our bodies get the energy they need to function at peak levels. Without good nutrition, a body's energy balance is broken, and it will look to other parts of its own systems to generate energy; this means we may feel lethargic, run-down, unfocused, or have difficulty sleeping at night, etc.

In short, proper nutrition provides the body with nutrients. Each food has certain nutrient densities. The healthier the food, the more nutrient dense it will be. It's those nutrients – like the high-octane fuel for a sports car – that power the machine we call the human body.

Proper nutrition helps us look, feel, and perform at our best. It allows us to accomplish what is most important to us without creating any imbalances in the body.

Proper nutrition is also sustainable. When practicing consuming optimal nutrition, we gain awareness of our food choices. We take note of what ingredients are in the food we eat, and we pay more attention to physical cues, such as how the body responds to some particular type of food. We take control of our mealtime surroundings, and more.

Proper nutrition also promotes regular movement and other healthy habits. When we focus on healthy nutritional choices, this can create awareness of other areas in our lives, including our physical fitness. When we're consuming truly nutritious foods that give our bodies the energy they need to function at peak levels, we tend to have a desire to be more physically active. There's a domino effect for our entire lives because we start to feel better from the inside-out, and we want to keep doing things that continue to make us feel amazing.

Additionally, proper nutrition is outcome-based. Every food choice you make will lead to a result, whether it's the result you want or not. If you eat potato chips, ice cream, or other unhealthy snacks all day long, then the results are most likely going to be weight gain, low energy levels, low motivation, emotional irregularities, poor mental focus, and a host of health issues down the road. On the flipside, if you have healthy nutritional habits, the outcome will most likely be the opposite.

The health of your body, both internal and external, showcases your decisions in everyday life. Yes, some people have health issues that affect their metabolism – causing weight gain, for example – that can make it harder for them to stay healthy or maintain their optimal weight. However, for the overwhelming majority of us, if we are overweight or unhealthy in other ways, it's often directly related to our nutrition or lack of activity.

Now, I would like you to meet Candice.

Meet Candice

When I first met Candice, she came to me with the desire for accountability via private workout sessions and a nutrition plan. She was a driven individual and the definition of a hard worker. As an extremely busy and successful lawyer, she often found herself putting in exceptionally long hours and barely getting up from her desk at her work.

Candice was a professional in every sense of the word. She was serious and your prototypical "straight shooter." She was in her late fifties, married, and had no children.

During her busy workdays, she would barely eat or drink anything most of the day. Talk about motivation and focus! With these long and busy days, she was getting almost no physical activity, and her energy levels were shot. However, once she returned home at night, she would often "gorge" (as she called it) on dinner. She would eat like she was actually starving.

On weekends, she would work part of the time and also enjoy dinners out with her husband or a few of her lady friends. She'd indulge in culinary masterpieces and select wines. And when it came to wine, she admitted to having more than one glass ... or two. Between Candace and her husband or her friends, they'd devour one or two full bottles, or sometimes more, depending on the company and how long they stayed at the restaurant.

As she told me about her lifestyle, one phrase kept popping into my mind: feast or famine. She was the perfect example of a feast-or-famine individual. She would "feast" on weeknights and on the weekends during social events but created "famine" in the day during work. She made work a priority over healthy nutrition.

What brought Candice to me was her recognizing the change in her body. As we move through our 40s, 50s, and beyond, the dietary habits we might have gotten away with in our 20s and 30s begin to catch up with us. While you might have been more physically active in your 20s and maybe even into your 30s, most people tend to become less active in their 40s and later.

Additionally, when we're younger, our bodies don't show the same level of change, including the same rate of weight gain, as when we move into, and through, our 40s and 50s. It's not that our metabolism has slowed because of age; it's because we're simply less active.

Women also have different hormonal stages in life. Our hormones can alter every time we have a child, and then of course prior to and during menopause. These changes make it harder for us to understand our bodies and how they respond to physical activity and nutrition.

People in their 40s and 50s are far less likely to get the same amount of physical activity as someone in their 20s or 30s. That's when our unhealthy dietary habits begin to catch up with us.

Candice noticed that. She recognized that her weight was increasing, she lacked energy, and she had trouble sleeping. She wasn't feeling like herself, as she described it to me.

Candice designated nutrition and physical activity as one of her top priorities moving forward. She wanted to create boundaries for her working hours, too. You see, she understood that something had to change. She wasn't pleased with the way things were progressing with her health, her body, her energy levels, and her unhealthy habits.

This is crucial for all of us. We need to be committed to change in order to see it truly happen within our lives and our bodies.

I sat down with Candice to go over her daily routines. She laid out her basic weekly schedule for me. It was quite a surprise to see how someone so driven to work such long hours barely made time for herself to eat or hydrate during the day. I was thankful we were on the "same page" about her situation.

Once she established realistic boundaries for her working hours, we mapped out a training schedule and a nutrition plan that would fit with schedule. I didn't want her sacrificing the quality of her work, and neither did she. I could tell she was very committed.

As a coach, I've had plenty of clients *say* they're committed, but then allow excuses to start to pop up. I get it. Life happens. Work and family responsibilities and life in general can get in the way. I totally understand and relate.

So, whenever you sit down to try to work out some type of regimen, some type of new schedule, always make sure it's realistic. Setting realistic goals is one of the keys to success! Don't try to add healthy habits to your schedule if you know they'll never work or that you'll only become more frustrated with your lack of progress.

Creating realistic goals in Candice's physical fitness and with her dietary habits was what she and I initially focused on. She set the boundaries for her working hours. I couldn't develop a training schedule for her without her first telling me those boundaries. For some people, getting exercise in the morning before work is the best option. For others, it might be during a one-hour lunch break. Still others may find the best consistency in the evening, or late at night when the kids are asleep.

Candice's work life wasn't all we had to address. Remember, her weekends were a social time of "letting go," throwing off the "shackles" of her work and being more carefree. I did recognize that her social life also needed a game plan. If she didn't take control of that splurging on fine meals, and the overconsumption of wine with her friends or spouse, then those weekends were going to make it hard for her to get back into her routine on Monday (not to mention making it impossible for her to lose weight).

Candice decided there were certain things she was willing to reduce. She would limit herself to one glass of wine at dinner instead of sharing a bottle or two with her company. She also decided to make conscious dinner choices. She'd look for the healthiest food items on the menu and choose from those options. She was also willing to take home left-overs from any meals that were beyond her appropriate portion size.

Portion control was a significant part of her journey. Once she understood that her inclination to eat everything on her plate was an unhealthy habit, and leftovers were a good idea because they'd allow her to have lunch for the next day, it became easier for her to justify only eating a reasonable portion of her meal.

These new changes in her attitude and outlook were small behavior changes. At first, they were things she had to really think about consciously, especially when she went out to dinner. That first weekend after we started her training schedule and her new dietary plan, she admitted it was difficult.

All of the old patterns had started grabbing at her, enticing her to let go and forget about it. "Just relax, unwind, and enjoy yourself," those little voices would tell her. "You deserve it!"

We all face this. That's why, when we decide to change certain aspects of our lives, we need to be aware of those feelings and emotions that arise and then make conscious choices that support the change we want to see within ourselves.

Verbally committing to something is easy, but it's a lot more difficult to put your words into action. This is completely normal. Think of an alcoholic trying to overcome their addiction; if they're in a social environment that has alcohol or in a household with family who drink, there is temptation; their willpower is constantly being tested.

If you, like Candice, have a pattern of feast or famine, not eating for long lengths of time and then overeating every time you sit down for a late-night dinner, there will be a temptation to simply dig in and throw caution to the wind.

Habits we want to develop are not going to happen by chance, though. Unhealthy habits can happen without us even realizing it, but the positive habits we want to develop to replace the old, unhealthy ones are going to require conscious, deliberate effort. For Candice, that meant staying focused every single time she went out to dinner, and especially during the weekends.

It's important that we set our own goals for such things rather than let someone else choose our goals for us. If I had told Candice she had to skip wine altogether, what would that have meant to her? Probably little to nothing. Why? It wasn't a goal that she wanted for herself. But I was not going to be with her at dinner. I would not have any clue whether she was having one glass or five. Her goal had to be something *she* truly wanted to strive for and stick to. Otherwise, it most likely wouldn't be sustainable.

This was a limit she set for herself, so when she'd go out, she had to make conscious decisions to sip on the one glass and switch to water once she was finished. Every time a temptation arose to have "just a little bit more," she'd again have to refocus on her behavior-based goals and the boundaries she'd set for herself.

Progress is a "fight," initiated in an effort to learn and attain new habits, until you have perfected your process and reached your ultimate goal. The more Candice experienced, the more she made the choices that would help her achieve her goals. When old, unhealthy habits tried to come back, she was forced to regroup and refocus, and she became better at controlling her temptations. As she maintained self-awareness and exercised healthy habits, she started to have more energy and see progress, which encouraged her to keep going and stay on a healthy path.

It is possible to perfect your process through behavior-based goals and reach your outcome-based goals. But it is going to be difficult if those goals have little to no meaning for you. That's why your goals must be deeply meaningful to you.

Candice had specific goals to get healthy and live a healthier lifestyle. This was meaningful to her. She didn't want to feel lethargic, low in energy, and she certainly didn't want to keep adding weight onto her body. She knew her daily routine was sending her down an unhealthy path. That's what brought her to me in the first place.

Anything worth fighting for will take effort and hard work to achieve. We will dive more into that later. Just understand this: If you are only going to focus on nutrition, exercise, or overall wellness because someone ridiculed you or said you had to, there's going to be very little meaning in it for you. Your superficial motivation will not be enough to push you through when times get tough. It must be something meaningful to you. And remember ... creating new habits takes time. This is not a race. It's about progress, not perfection.

Takeaways from Candice

Candice had been so focused on her career that she developed habits leading to an unhealthy lifestyle. But fortunately, even before we sat down to work together, she was committed to making the necessary changes. More importantly, she knew what was deeply meaningful to her.

Often, I meet potential clients who have no idea what goals they want to set or what they want their future to look like. Too often, people set goals for the wrong reasons. It may be for vain reasons, perhaps because someone made a statement that made them feel bad about themselves or they saw a celebrity and wanted to look like them.

Are those compelling enough reasons for someone to create permanent change? They could be, but not usually. As I've mentioned already, the reason for changing needs to be personally meaningful to you if you are searching for long-term change.

Candice's desire to change her lifestyle was meaningful. She didn't want to carry the extra weight or add more weight, and she didn't like how her low energy levels made her feel because they affected her entire day. She also didn't want to feel guilty on Sunday evenings when she looked back and recognized that she'd gone a little overboard and the workweek was about to begin again.

Candice asked herself the hard questions that many people try to avoid, and she sought to understand what goals were meaningful to her. When she approached me, those goals were already in mind. She just didn't know how she was going to get there. This was where my experience, expertise, and ability to help others came into play.

You need to have a keen awareness of what your goals are. This is an essential aspect of making progress of any kind. I've worked with clients like Candice who knew very well what their goals were, right from the beginning, and I've also worked with others who only had vague notions. With the latter, I work with my clients to help them define their meaningful goals that aligned with their lifestyles. We'll cover this more in detail later.

For you, the question now is this: *What are the exercise and nutrition obstacles in your life?* Do you tend to gorge on food later in the day because you've skipped breakfast and lunch? Do you intend to go to the gym early in the morning before your family wakes up, but end up hitting the snooze button instead? Do you tend to sneak the cookies that you bought for your kids when everyone else is asleep? Find those obstacles and confront them; only then can you overcome them.

So, let's find out what those exercise and nutrition obstacles are in your life.

Self-Discovery: Your Activities List

This activity involves two aspects: the body and nutrition.

The Body

First, list all of the activities you currently engage in. You might be thinking, "Renee, I don't really do any activities." Well, you do. Guess what? You're currently reading this book. That's one activity. The activities we're talking about don't have to require physical exertion or be considered working out. They could be work-related. Maybe you drive yourself to work every day. That's an activity. Maybe you sit in a cubicle all day crunching numbers. That's an activity. Everything you do on a somewhat-regular basis counts. Your answers don't have to be health-related. Just list them. You'll find that your list will end up being quite long.

Second, list the activities you would like to do (separate from your first list). This could be anything, realistic or unrealistic. If you'd love to run a major city marathon in two years, write that down. If you'd like to start paddleboarding or kayaking, write it down. If you want to start taking walks with your family, put that on your list. Whatever it is you want to do, write it down.

Third, after you've completed that list, I want you to list all of the activities that you would **realistically** do from your second list. You see, this is going to be much different. This should be a list of things that are realistic, at least at this point in your life.

Do your best to refrain from oversimplifying and deciding that none of the activities are realistic. This typically means that nothing on your list is deeply meaningful to you. If you find this is the case, go back to step two and take the time to recreate your list with things that are truly meaningful to you. If it is important to you, you'll find a way to make it work with your schedule.

Fourth, note how often you will do these activities each week. What time duration will you allow for them? At what time in the day will you do them? Where? Would you do these activities with someone else or solo? If so, who?

Lastly, create an alternative scenario for those activities you plan to realistically do, including a different time, day, or place. In case Plan A doesn't work out for one reason or another, you'll have a Plan B.

All of these lists force you to filter out "likes" versus "needs" and "unrealistic" versus "realistic." You now have a better gauge on what's meaningful to you and what's realistic to you.

Nutrition

For the nutritional aspect of this activity, start by listing the foods you regularly consume. Include items that are in your rotation multiple times per day, daily, multiple times per week, and/or weekly. This list may become long, so do your best to be as detailed as possible.

Second, do your best to mark which items are healthy and which are unhealthy. Some of your food options may be a little more obvious, like fruits and vegetables, in general, are healthy. (Please note that the accuracy of this statement will vary depending on the selected fruit and its consumption frequency. Some fruits contain high levels of natural sugar.) Food options that tend to be unhealthy would be things like cookies, cakes, chips, etc.

If you are unsure about whether something is healthy or unhealthy, but the food item has a nutritional label, check it out and review each element. Without diving too deeply into the details of a nutritional facts label, in general, unhealthy macronutrients we would like to keep as low as possible for health are trans-unsaturated fats (or trans-fatty acids), cholesterol, sodium, sugar, and artificial sweeteners.

Similarly, limiting your saturated fat intake is recommended. Keep in mind that some research suggests that certain saturated fats, such as medium-chain triglycerides (MCTs) and stearic acid (a long-chain fatty acid), may have neutral or potentially beneficial effects when consumed in moderation.

In general, healthy macronutrients include unsaturated fats, such as monounsaturated and polyunsaturated fats, as well as protein, fiber, and total carbohydrates (depending on the source).

Notice the serving size, total calories, and whether the ingredients list is filled with unfamiliar words or more whole-food ingredients.

Once you have gained more insight into the foods you typically consume, it will be easier to determine whether the items on your list are helping you achieve your goals or potentially moving you further away from them.

Third, can you take any unhealthy food items from your list and replace them with a healthier version? If you're not sure, that's okay. This is not a quiz to test your knowledge of nutrition, but if you know right away that something on your list has a healthier alternative (many do), write that alternative down next to it.

For example, let's say you typically buy Oroweat 100% Whole Grain bread with larger slices. Instead of completely eliminating bread from your diet, consider replacing it with one slice of Dave's 21 Whole Grains and Seeds bread, which has smaller slices. This simple swap alone removes: 70 calories, 2g of fat, 85 mg of sodium, and 9 grams of carbohydrates, including 1g of sugar.

Take the time to seek out healthier alternatives for your favorite foods that are unhealthy and holding you back. A quick internet search may help you discover other options. This exercise will create awareness for places where your meals could instantly improve and become healthier!

Strive for progress, not perfection.

Next, we're going to bring the spirit of your being into play in order to help enact long-lasting, positive change.

"Remember: food is fuel, not therapy." — Unknown

The Strength of the Spirit

"As you live your values, your sense of identity, integrity, control, and inner-focus will infuse you with both exhilaration and peace. You will define yourself from within, rather than by people's opinions or by comparisons to others." — Stephen R. Covey

What is the spirit? Depending on your upbringing, culture, belief system, or ideology, a person's spirit can mean many different things. Generally speaking, when talking about personal change, motivation, and moving in a new, positive direction in life, our "spirit" generally encapsulates our system of values, our soul, and the collective nature of our being.

I am not a shaman or a guru. I'm not someone who's going to lead you in a spiritual sense, but I do recognize how instrumental and vital the spirit is for long-lasting change.

Just as the body without the mind is simply an empty vessel and the mind without the body is inexpressible, a body without a spirit is just a robot. A mind without its companion spirit becomes nothing more than an animal surviving on instinct.

If it were simply about instinct and survival, our world would be a much different place. We would never marvel at the beauty of sunsets or look out across the ocean and contemplate our own place on this planet or in the universe.

You are vital. *You are important.* You are a part of what makes this entire universe the most amazing creation one could ever imagine. And you are more than just your body. You are more than just your mind. You are the entirety of your mind, body, and spirit.

Your Innate Spirit

Many people consider the spirit of a person to be rooted in the components that they believe make up morality. For example, what you believe, how you help others in a time of need, how you focus on staying motivated in life, or anything that comprises your moral fabric. Spiritually, we each maintain a system of values guiding the soul or the discerning mind, which, in turn, makes countless judgments and choices all the time.

The spiritual part of a person is regarded as a moral aspect. This is a vital principle of a conscious life for human beings. It is this spiritual component of a person that separates us from all other animals. Yes, imagination and the ability to dream a future that has not yet been written is part of that. But, where do ideas for new developments, new creations, and new designs come from?

I want you to embrace the spiritual aspect of your journey. No matter what your fundamental beliefs about creation, God, karma, self-empowerment, or anything else, understand this: The spiritual aspect of a person and the moral foundation that comprises the essence of a person is crucial to long-lasting change.

For human beings, the spirit is a vital principle in the conscious life. You and I may never have met personally, but I can tell you that your spirit is beautiful. How do I know this? Because you recognize just how amazing this gift of life is and you desire to take advantage of all it has to offer. You want to honor this gift by taking better care of yourself and by moving things in a different direction, away from unhealthy choices.

A person can change their mind, and they can even start changing their body. But if they neglect their spirit – which enables them to gain true insight into themselves, their mindset, and their understanding of their family or health – then that change may not endure over time. It may be short-lived.

Fads Fade

As I have mentioned, there are plenty of weight loss plans out there. They've come and gone like the changing of seasons. Here today, gone tomorrow. People latch onto something that gains traction in the public view and become excited about it. Then, they chase after it, buy into the program, and begin shedding some excess weight.

Then what?

Many revert to their previous habits, regaining lost weight and, unfortunately, sometimes surpassing their initial starting point.

Fads, or trends, do not tend to encapsulate mind, body, and spirit, which are critical to long-term change. Lasting change rooted in something deeply meaningful will positively upgrade your life and lead to increased levels of confidence and self-esteem, as well as create a healthy lifestyle that is sustainable.

In essence, change is not a fleeting trend but a profound journey, acknowledging the intricacies of the mind, body, and spirit. Embracing this interconnected perspective steers individuals toward a path of vibrancy, confidence, and fulfillment. This transformative journey is an opportunity to celebrate the uniqueness of each step toward personal health and well-being.

Meet Lori

Lori came to me with a completely different purpose and priority, at least when compared to Candice and Allison. She was a kind, quiet, level-headed individual in her 40s, and a busy mother of two children.

When we sat down for the first time, she expressed what was driving her to change her life by getting fit and starting to eat healthier. It was not about her. At least, not all of it. It was more for her kids.

She was noticing her children gaining weight. They'd all taken on unhealthy habits. They were eating the wrong foods, and getting less and less exercise, and it was beginning to show. In fact, according to Lori, this trend had been developing over time. What she began to recognize were the results of their unhealthy habits, which were affecting more than just their weight.

Both of her children were becoming more introverted. They seemed to have lower self-esteem, less confidence, and were feeling ashamed. She was devastated. She was *heartbroken*. Yet, no matter what she tried to do to lift their spirits, to help them feel better, smile more, and laugh more, nothing seemed to work.

Her children had started withdrawing, spending less time with friends, and talking less about their experiences at school. She could only imagine the things other kids might be saying to them and worried that this was just the beginning.

Lori went through a period of extreme sadness and guilt. She believed this was her fault, that her poor food choices and lack of exercise had inspired them to follow suit. Her lack of teaching them how to take better care of themselves, be more active, and eat healthier foods had created this situation.

The reality was, Lori could empathize with her children. She, too, had gained weight. She was also feeling less confident about herself and in her own skin. Her self-esteem was moving to an all-time low. On top of her own shrinking self-image, she felt she had failed as a parent.

Most parents want the best for their children. Some people think this means giving their children everything they want; others recognize the importance of discipline and teaching children through their own actions as good role models.

Children learn from our actions. Ever see a social media video of a toddler trying to do push-ups or burpees? Yeah, that wasn't by accident. They were most likely copying one of their parents.

Lori was making unhealthy food choices, which caused her to have less energy and resulted in a decline in her physical activity. Her children were following suit.

When it comes to parenting, the "do as I say, not as I do" approach rarely works. Children can see right through hypocrisy. Lori was living proof that our children, ultimately, end up doing the things we do, regardless of what we tell them.

She was feeling guilty about this, but while that certainly led her to me, it's important you understand that guilt is a self-inflicted emotion. Guilt tends to be an anchor that pulls us down. You expend all your limited energy just trying to get through one more day with that anchor weighing you down.

If you're like Lori and feel guilty because someone has been impacted by your unhealthy choices, whether directly or indirectly, allow that emotion to motivate you to move toward change; then, let it go. Let that guilt slip away from you. Don't cling onto it anymore. Remember, guilt mostly does one thing: it keeps us looking backward. You cannot possibly move forward effectively if you are always focused on looking back.

Try to accept that this feeling of guilt led you to a much better place – one of awareness – which is a good thing.

Lori knew she had to change her unhealthy habits into healthy ones, for herself as well as for her children. It was not just about her; if her children didn't learn healthy habits before they went off to college, or moved out and started their own lives as adults, they'd carry these unhealthy habits along with them through life.

It's a lot easier for a parent to *show* their child healthy habits than to let their child go out on their own and try to learn from a world full of marketing designed to lead them to unhealthy choices.

At this stage in her life, it was extremely important to Lori to become a better role model for her entire family. She knew if she could change her unhealthy habits into healthy ones, then there'd be a sincere desire among her children to want to follow suit.

Lori wanted to make staying active fun. Living a healthy lifestyle should be enjoyable. Doing this as a family brings everyone together. It stimulates these bonds that are so unique to families, especially between parents and their children. When you create a strong bond through activities like exercising, playing sports, or preparing healthy meals together, you create positive memories.

For Lori, her starting point was herself. She knew she couldn't force her children to modify their habits until she worked on her own habits first. That's why she signed up to work with me, and we developed a healthy plan designed specifically for her.

As a parent preparing meals for her children, her new, healthy nutrition plan would immediately benefit her children. She might not be able to control everything her children ate for lunch at school. Even breakfast at home was always rushed and quick while everyone got ready for the day. But dinners were a good starting point for her to begin transitioning her family away from unhealthy choices to healthy ones that would (hopefully) develop into habits.

As time progressed, she started to get her kids involved in helping to prepare some of those meals, which is a wonderful learning opportunity for children, no matter their age. When kids help you prepare healthy meals in the kitchen, you can teach them healthy habits and have a bonding experience that creates positive memories. Your family, as a support system, grows stronger.

The more time Lori spent preparing these meals together with her children, the more her kids learned and absorbed. And the more excited they became, too – especially when they were able to sit down and savor the nutritious meal they'd created together. That sense of achievement builds a child's self-esteem and confidence.

After a while, Lori began noticing that her children were starting to make healthier snack choices for themselves. They did this without any prompting from her. She didn't have to tell them, "Why don't you have some berries instead of those cookies?" They were taking the initiative and doing it on their own.

Because they were learning and wanted to emulate Mom, who was also making healthier choices.

Her children also started initiating family-time activities. In the beginning, there was significant resistance, but then, instead of her asking them if they wanted to go to the park or take a walk, they were the ones asking her to do these things. Lori felt fortunate and thankful she had made the decision to be proactive about her entire family's health.

One day, seemingly out of the blue, Lori's daughter expressed an interest in joining her during the private workout sessions she had with me. Lori messaged me to see if that would be okay, and my response was "Of course."

They ended up having many sessions together with me. I was blessed to witness the bond that was growing and strengthening between them. They enjoyed each other's company and, just as importantly, they motivated one another to keep going. While they grew stronger physically, they also grew stronger emotionally and spiritually, and did it together. Their support for each other was incredible. I found myself being inspired by them.

When you start focusing on healthy lifestyle choices one day at a time, the network of people in your life who can be motivated and inspired to live a healthier lifestyle silently grows. You might not see the results. But understand that taking these initial steps is not only going to improve *your* life, *your* outlook on life, and *your* self-esteem and confidence levels; sharing your journey can also impact your children, spouse, friends, co-workers, and even people you may not have met yet via social media.

Lori was blessed to see that firsthand with her own children. And I believe that, eventually, her children will show others these healthy habits. The lives they are going to positively influence, because of this experience, is going to increase Lori's impact.

Remember this. Your impact is going to continue to expand exponentially, even if you don't realize it's happening.

After many months of us working together, Lori told me her children were consistently more active, and losing weight, and that their attitudes and dispositions had changed for the better. They were happy, confident, proud, and more outgoing.

Along this journey, Lori experienced the same transformation as they did. It was as though she was becoming a completely new person – born again, as one might say – and enjoying a closer personal relationship with her children.

Lori's children were her deeply meaningful purpose for getting healthy. She was so passionate about them, and that drive kept her focused and on-track.

It was her spirit that had needed reviving. Her day-to-day routine had distracted her from what was truly important to her: her family; having healthy, higher standards for herself so that she could be a good role model; showing love and acceptance to herself; and not taking for granted all of the blessings she had, such as moments with her family.

Being a parent is one of the hardest but most rewarding jobs there is. You have the opportunity to mold the mind of a young person's life so that they'll take the path of goodness, success, and fulfillment. You cannot control everything that happens to them. You cannot control every decision they will ultimately make. But, you lay a foundation for living a healthy lifestyle, that will resonate with them as they move into and through their adult lives, and ultimately pass it on to anyone they are close with.

Whether you are a parent or not, you are a role model for someone. Maybe you are an aunt, uncle, sister, brother, or even someone on social media who provides daily inspiration, etc. For better or for worse, the people who idolize you will look to you for how to act, think, believe, and even feel.

Sometimes, it's our family that creates the self-awareness and willingness in us, to do whatever it takes for them. This can start us on a journey of long-lasting transformation. That, my friends, is true love.

Takeaways from Lori

There are so many things that we can take away from Lori's story, but the one I want you to focus on is simply this: Spiritually, Lori instinctively had awareness, insight, empathy, and understanding for what her children were experiencing. Through her system of values and morals, she was able to make a positive judgment call for the actionable steps that would improve the lives of her children.

Lori was driven to make some form of change due to initial guilt over how her children were living, looking, and feeling. Her meaningful purpose was to be a better role model for her children.

Personal, deep meaning is at the heart of change. Having high moral fiber entails caring about yourself and others to the highest degree possible. It's a moral foundation rooted in your spirit, your soul, and the essence of everything you are.

No matter what you are striving for, or what journey you are on, when you develop healthy habits and achieve the goals you set out for yourself, the depths to which you will positively impact others have no limits! You will inspire!

Take a moment to reflect on your morals and values – the things that make you unique and guide your spirit and mind. I encourage you to write these thoughts down and keep the notes where you can glance at them often as a reminder. Honoring this spiritual part of you is important for long-term personal improvement and fulfillment.

Never forget just how marvelous you are and the positive influence you can have on so many other people ... even the ones you may never have actually met.

Source: billionairesquotess.blogspot.com[30]

Self-Discovery: Ready? Set. Goals!

We are creatures of habit. It is important to create the right action steps for yourself and define the new habits you believe will be effective in altering your behavior.

It's also critical to create a workable plan. As I touched on in the previous Self-Discovery Activity, you may have things you would like to do, but which aren't (yet) realistic.

Your plan must be workable. It must be doable. If you're working 50 or 60 hours a week and raising children, planning a trip to your local gym every day isn't likely feasible. It's not realistically workable.

While your ambitions and goals might be as high as Mount Everest, you need to make them workable. It's better to start with smaller plans, with something that's not going to completely upend your entire life at this stage in the game – the one that starts your path of transformation. Creating smaller steps will ensure you're far more likely to stick to the plan rather than if the overall, larger goal is your actual focus.

Reflecting on the current goals you have for yourself and using the answers you discovered from the last Self-Discover Activity, I'd like you to answer two questions on the next page.

Be honest with yourself. Only you will know the answers. Have fun with it and truly explore deep within yourself. What answers do your mind, body, and spirit tell you? These first two questions can be written down or simply reflected upon.

Question #1: Are you ready?

It's a simple question. Are you ready for this change that you desire? Is this something you truly and deeply want in your life? Is it extremely meaningful to you?

If you answered no to any of those questions, that's okay. Understanding you are not truly ready is very important. Never rush your goals. Only begin striving for them and putting in the work once your mindset is truly ready.

Most people who tackle their goals before they're truly ready end up quitting when things get tough. Look no further than traditional New Year's resolutions to understand what I mean.

According to a study carried out at the University of Scranton, around 80% of New Year's resolutions are unsuccessful by the second week of February. Likewise, a research article published in *The Journal of Clinical Psychology* discovered that merely 46% of people can sustain their resolutions beyond the six-month point, and only approximately 8% of people are successful in achieving their resolutions.[31]

So, are you truly ready?

Question #2: What's holding you back?

If you answered no to the first question, reflect in order to understand what's holding you back. If this change is truly meant for you, and if you are motivated to see this transformation in your life, *what's* been holding you back?

There are no wrong answers to any of these questions. The point is to be more open and honest with yourself. This will give you better clarity so you can address potential obstacles as they jump up and try to drag you back – because they will, at least in the beginning.

Once you understand what's holding you back, follow up by asking yourself, *why* is this holding me back from working towards my goals?

Is it because of scheduling issues, lack of motivation, lack of resources, no accountability or support system, or something else? Once you know the reason, you can properly adapt or change your goal to make it more workable and/or meaningful.

Now, for your Self-Discover Activity.

Write three meaningful goals in your life for each of the below categories:

- Mental/Emotional
- Physical/Nutritional
- Spiritual

Then, take some time to place them in order of importance ... for you. This is not a matter of importance to me or where you think I (or anyone else in your life) would place them, but for yourself, your life, and your ideology.

Save this list for now. We will work on this list more in a just bit.

Part 3

Finding What's Deeply Meaningful

"The heart of human excellence often begins to beat when you discover a pursuit that absorbs you, frees you, challenges you, or gives you a sense of meaning, joy, or passion." — Terry Orlick

"Why am I here?"

This is perhaps, above all others, *the* quintessential question of every person alive. Anyone who has conscious thought will, has, or will *again* – at some point in their life – ask this question or a similar version of it.

"Why am I here?"

There are about as many different layers to this question as there are answers. Yet, when you grind away all the grit of life, the core of this question gets to who you are as a person, and *what matters most* ... to you.

In other words, you are digging down to your purpose.

Everyone has a purpose. I have a purpose, and you most definitely have a purpose. Currently, you may not be aligned with your true meaning, that one thing which is invariably your most deep and meaningful purpose. If this is the case, stress, frustration, doubt, and feelings of hopelessness may resonate with you, while a sense of self-worth may not.

Inside, deep down in the heart of who you are, where that small voice speaks to you throughout the day or late at night when you can't sleep, *your purpose is calling to you.*

Maybe you fully understand your purpose, but for one reason or another, you're not fulfilling it. Maybe you *understand* your purpose, but don't feel you have the means to pursue whatever it is.

Let me tell you right now: *You do.*

You are powerful. As I have said before, and as I will say again and again until it is ingrained into your mind: *You are AMAZING!* You are the only person like you in the world. Even if you are an identical twin or one of triplets, you are not entirely the same as your siblings.

You are unique because you are the product of not just your genetics or your biology, but your choices, your experiences, your dreams, and your ideas for the future.

You are also the product of the family that nurtured you in your youth, the family you later create, the friends you choose, your career, and more.

That is what makes you an incredible and quite unique person.

What I have noticed while working with many unique people is that very few of us dig down deep to understand our true purpose, to embrace that purpose, to use it to help motivate us, and to empower us to make the right choices when we're confronted with difficulties.

Maybe that crossroad is you needing to choose whether to have a delicious chocolate chip cookie that you don't need but are craving because some stressor in your life is triggering an emotional response.

Those choices matter.

Yes, some choices are obvious and can affect the course of our lives in tremendous ways, but those small ones – the seemingly inconsequential choices that we typically don't pay close attention to – can also have lasting repercussions.

The small drip of a faucet may not seem to be a big deal, but if the drain is clogged, the sink will fill. When the sink fills, it can overflow.

When it overflows, water can seep down into the floor and walls, rot the foundation of a home, and eventually even collapse a house.

What I want you to focus on right now is finding your true purpose. And yes, we can have more than one purpose in life.

Turn your energy toward digging deep down to figure out what is *most* deeply meaningful to you. What is your deeply meaningful purpose at this stage in your life?

Triumph Over Harmful Behaviors

When you have a clear picture of what your true purpose is, that understanding will help you overcome just about any harmful behavior because you will have more direction.

An example of a harmful behavior in this context might be grabbing snacks in a moment when you're not truly hungry, but rather stressed, or choosing to sit down rather than exercising simply because the day felt brutal, and you want to decompress by doing absolutely nothing.

After a while, you may feel as though you are trapped, hopeless, and beyond redemption because of your weight or your addiction, but *you are not*. You are the most unique individual in the world, no one is like you, and you are amazing and powerful.

Keep telling yourself, "I. Am. Amazing. I. Have. The. Power."

It doesn't matter how you may have felt in the past, or even how you've been feeling before starting to read this section. You may have felt despair – like nothing has ever worked for you and probably ever will.

This is the moment where everything changes.

This is the moment when you start to discover your purpose.

I want you to imagine, as you read this, that you are sitting in your favorite room within your home. There's a camera on you. You are watching yourself. The camera moves back and away. You recognize the same three walls (the fourth wall is obviously behind the camera). You notice the items in the room.

Suddenly, the camera glides backward and slips through metal bars. This is something you've never noticed before: You're in a prison. The cell door is closed and locked. But as the camera continues to pull away, you see an object – a hook on the wall that's within reach. A key. The key to your cell is dangling right there. With a little effort, that key will set you free from your unhealthy mindset and habits.

Right now, you may be feeling as though nothing has ever worked and nothing will ever help you achieve your goals.

Your life might feel like that prison.

The door may be locked, but the key is within reach. You have full access to that key. Now, you must decide whether you're going to remain there or get up, reach through the bars, grab the key, and set yourself free once and for all.

I am here to help you make your great escape.

Your Vision + Mission

"When a person can't find a deep sense of meaning, they distract themselves with pleasure." — Viktor E. Frankl

Everyone has a purpose. Everyone has a meaning for why they are here, alive, at this moment.

Regardless of the past, your future is unwritten. It is full of potential and possibility.

One way to find your purpose is by, first, refraining from measuring yourself against others. You know the saying: "That's like comparing apples to oranges." There's no one like you who has the *exact* same genetics, upbringing, experiences, learned skills, innate talents, injuries, health status, and so forth.

All of these elements and more have brought you to where you are in life and helped you evolve into the person you are today. Your mind, body, and spirit are unique to you. So, when you start comparing yourself to others, consciously or subconsciously, it's not an accurate comparison.

When we compare ourselves to others in the gym, we're more inclined to compare ourselves to others who are more fit than we think we are. In doing this, we're setting unrealistic expectations for ourselves. It's easier to find reasons for quitting than to see that fit person and be motivated to put in the effort to become just as fit.

No two people – in a gym or any other environment – are alike. So, be kind to yourself and give yourself a chance to succeed. Your healthy life is within reach, but anything worth having will require some effort.

There are plenty of people whose most important purpose in life is to have children, raise them, and provide the best opportunities for them. They couldn't imagine anything more meaningful to them. There are others who find their career to be the most meaningful thing in their life.

Fulfillment is achieved when you are living your life's purpose.

Your vision, mission, and goals are what helps you achieve and live your purpose, which might look one way when you're 16 years old, and then look different at 30 or 45 years of age.

If you're a parent with children still at home, you'll likely turn to a different vision, mission, or goals once your children head off to college or begin their adult lives away from home. You're still going to support your children, but you'll have finished preparing them for the best opportunity possible in the real world.

To understand what your real purpose is, personal self-reflection must happen for you, and not be attached to anyone else. Once you know your purpose, you can create behavior-based goals that will allow you to reach your purpose.

Do not judge yourself about what you discover when you dig deep. Part of the process is to grind away the grit of life to find what's deeply meaningful to you. It may be relatively straightforward, but if you're always seeking to please others, you may find yourself pursuing a purpose that's not truly meaningful to you.

Let this be about you and only you. If your children are the most deeply meaningful thing to you, great. If it's your career, wonderful. If it's about getting in shape, eating healthier, or anything else – fantastic. But do not let being a parent or caring for others deter you from something else in your life that fulfills your unique purpose.

You might need to use that last sentence as a mantra of sorts:

"I will not let being a parent or caring for others deter me from something else in my life that fulfills my unique purpose."

Your meaningful purpose must be genuine. If it's not, it becomes much more difficult for you to overcome harmful behaviors and inevitable temptations that come your way.

When you ask yourself the hard questions in order to understand your vision and mission, do not be superficial. Never align yourself with a purpose because you want to "look better" or because someone you know (or even a random celebrity) has given you a generalized notion of what it could feel like to lose weight or follow some other random goal. Avoid the superficial and aim for the meaningful.

If you focus on the superficial and it's not meaningful to you, the odds you will quit increase exponentially. This is one of the reasons so many fad diets come and go; the fitness regimens, the exercise videos, and so forth tend to do very little for people in the long-term. Yes, many of these plans can help in the short-term, but because the individuals who start them never actually dug below the surface to what is truly meaningful to them, the fads often fall away.

That is what this book is really about: the long-lasting change that we want to see in our lives. And in order for us to enact long-lasting change, it cannot be superficial.

Meet Rosa

For Rosa, one of the biggest challenges was caring for her special-needs son. She had two sons, but one required around-the-clock care.

Rosa was a driven, determined professional who worked for a large corporation. She put in incredibly long hours and was someone with constant dedication and integrity. Everything she did was for the benefit of her family. Rosa had a demanding life, and her exceptionally busy schedule was written all over her face; pure exhaustion.

When it came to her children, she was your prototypical mother. The "mama bear" willing to do anything to protect her "cubs." But when one of your children requires constant care, it's extremely easy to feel overwhelmed.

On top of that need, Rosa had multiple health issues of her own which limited her mobility. When we first met, she admitted that on most mornings, she had trouble simply getting out of bed due to pain. If she had to pick something up from the floor, she didn't know if she would be able to straighten back up.

She was in constant pain, struggling to get through each day. Those ailments were compromising her ability to get everything done that her life demanded of her. She came to me because she didn't know what else to do.

Some people have the mental capacity to set aside the pain, stress, and anxiety of a specific moment, knowing that other people are counting on them. This ability to focus even to one's physical detriment is only temporary and can often lead to other outlets for relief that aren't typically healthy.

Even though things were getting tougher and tougher for Rosa, she kept pressing on. Her children needed her, especially her son. Her other child was considered "normal," but that did not mean things were always easy. Rosa struggled with stress, worry, and guilt. She wanted to focus on her son in every moment she wasn't at work, but the physical toll was making it extremely difficult.

She was so overwhelmed throughout her busy day that there didn't seem to be any time for her to reflect on the routinely unhealthy habits she'd developed. Her nights felt as scattered as her days. Most nights, her sleep was broken and she barely managed three uninterrupted hours of sleep. The rest of the night was usually spent tossing and turning, drifting off halfway and then waking up with thoughts and worries still spiraling around in her mind.

With her being constantly stressed out and exhausted, focusing on staying hydrated was not a priority; she drank caffeinated beverages to keep moving. Her diet often consisted of snacks and grab-and-go meals. This didn't offer her body any reliable or consistent nutrition. Nor did it offer the kind of energy she needed to get through her days.

By the time she reached out to me, Rosa had already asked herself some tough questions. She'd come to realize that if she was going to be able to help her son appropriately, she first needed to focus on herself.

That's a great mentality to have. If you're not taking care of yourself, then all of your efforts, all of your dedication, can slip away, especially if you find yourself facing a serious health issue that makes it virtually impossible for you to help others.

Rosa realized this and recognized that her first priority had to be her own health.

Was that her deeply meaningful purpose? No, she felt her meaningful purpose was being there for her son to attend to his constant need for care. She believed that God had made him her son for a reason – because she was strong, driven, and caring. But in order to be the best mom she could be, she had to make her health a top priority.

Rosa knew where she was falling short. She was determined to focus on self-care with her overarching goal of being able to take better care for her family.

Our initial meetings were challenging. Her motherly instinct kept wanting to kick in. She kept wanting to default to her old habits, to focus first on her son and neglect her own self-care.

During our sessions, her eyes constantly wandered back to her smartphone to check for notifications. That made it quite difficult for her to begin forging new, healthy habits that were designed to focus on her first. Mothers often think it's selfish to want to focus on improving themselves or practicing self-care. They're so focused on their feelings of guilt that it's almost impossible to acknowledge how changing focus to their own well-being will truly benefit others, especially their family, in the long run.

But the best thing you can do for those you love is to take better care of yourself. This way, you can give them the best version of you.

I think about elderly couples who go through their entire lives together. Maybe one gets a medical diagnosis, and their partner is suddenly tasked with the primary responsibility of taking care of them. I'm talking about the kind of care which physically, emotionally, and mentally takes a toll on a person. Yet, that spouse never thinks twice about whether they can continue doing it.

That is love.

Like Rosa, make yourself a priority so that you can start working on fulfilling the purpose you've defined for yourself. Notice, I didn't say you should make yourself your *only* priority. This doesn't mean neglecting your other priorities. It's not one or the other. We're simply adding to what you're going to be focusing on. And in that case, there's no logical reason to be hard on yourself or react with guilt.

I scheduled regular private fitness sessions with Rosa, and this held her accountable. Rosa didn't miss a single session, and that was a great start. Even though there were plenty of times when she felt like she should be home with her son after a long day at work, she was good about reminding herself that attending our sessions was the right thing to do for her family.

Together, we worked to create a nutrition plan that would support her extremely busy, on-the-go lifestyle and routine.

I've seen individuals with insanely busy lives, but Rosa's schedule and responsibilities humbled and inspired me. Compared to her, I felt like I was standing still.

The Battles are Not the War

For our purposes, "the war" is to eat healthy, stay active, and reach our own optimal health. Within every war are battles.

As with any journey, Rosa's had its share of battles. Well, they were more like quarrels. In the beginning, Rosa seemed to fight me at every turn. She kept wanting to turn back to the more comfortable and easier alternatives, to habits that had led her to this moment in the first place. Eventually, though, her resistance began to diminish. She started developing routines and noticed progress, which influenced her to trust and follow the process.

In a short time, our training sessions began to positively affect her life. It became easier for Rosa to get out of bed in the morning. That was one of the first things she noticed, as she mentioned to me one day with a big smile on her face. Also, picking up something off the floor and getting back up was now doable. Pain that had been chronic was beginning to relent. (For anyone who has endured seemingly never-ending pain, that is a miraculous blessing!)

Rosa noticed she had more energy when she spent time with her children. Her outlook on life, especially about herself and her situation, had gone from being discouraged to being hopeful and more confident.

It was a powerful transition for me to witness. And that is one of the things that gets me moving in the morning – knowing someone is going to experience that kind of transition from the guidance I offer. That is one of *my* deeply meaningful purposes.

Rosa recognized that she was also treating people better. She was able to help her son more effectively, being there more regularly when he needed her, even if it was at all hours of the night. Her positive attitude trickled down to the rest of her family.

But it all started with her personal, meaningful purpose. Having that deeply meaningful purpose well-defined for yourself is going to give you the power to overcome the moments when you want to fight against what's new and return to those old, comfortable self-sabotaging habits.

That's the most amazing thing about this kind of journey: When you focus and strive to reach your purpose which fulfills you, you affect not just yourself and those in your immediate circle, but cause repercussions well beyond that.

Takeaways from Rosa

One thing I have noticed in all of my years spent helping people pursue their goals, especially when it comes to overall wellness, is that most people focus on the outcome-based goals that they *think* are important without taking the time to "dig deep" and uncover their own most profound purpose.

If you are focused on the goals that are not rooted in something profoundly meaningful to you, the odds of falling short, or quitting altogether, increase dramatically.

Looking at this infographic, you can probably recognize some of these reasons *why people give up.*[32] Just look back on some of the goals you've set for yourself – whether work-related, nutrition-focused, activity-related, or anything else. Think back on those times when you had goals and didn't quite achieve them. What was missing?

WHY PEOPLE GIVE UP
expect fast results
stop believing in themselves
get stuck in the past
dwell on mistakes
fear the future
resist change
give up their power
believe in their weaknesses
feel the world owes them something
fear failure more than desire success
never visualize what is possible
feel they have something to lose
overwork
assume their problems are unique
see failure as the signal to turn back
feel sorry for themselves

If you don't connect your goals to something truly meaningful to you, you may come up with an army of excuses to rationalize why quitting is a good option.

This is one of the main reasons why most New Year's resolutions fall by the wayside within a matter of weeks. People love the *idea* of changing certain aspects of their lives, especially when it comes to things they're not happy with, but what's the driving motivator? Usually, it's what we think others perceive of us.

So, the thought of new habits for a new year is exciting and creates hope but is often short-lived. This is common with most people who decide to attempt a new habit: They want to start at the new year, or at the start of a new month (or even a new week).

The easiest way to spot someone who has good intentions but isn't truly ready, or isn't doing it for the right reasons, is to see when they plan to start. If they're waiting for a new year, new month, or new week, they're not ready. A person who is truly ready to put the effort into creating new habits, or doing it for the right reasons, will start right away once they make the decision to change. There's no waiting.

There's another reason most New Year's resolutions fall by the wayside. The excitement for change and possibility is so strong that people try to change *everything* at once – for instance, to work out five times a week and adopt a restrictive nutritional plan (without any idea of what it should look like). Also, they want to practice regular meditation, consume a gallon of water each day, read more books, sleep more, and work on stress management. All this does is create *more* stress. It's too much, too soon. Most people try to tackle all of this on their own simply because "it's a new year," even when they haven't taken the time to look at their schedule or daily routines to see if their goals are even realistic.

The expectations were set so high that they've only set themselves up for falling short. Then, the psychological implications affect their self-esteem, confidence, and ability to practice self-love. This simply becomes a vicious circle.

Before you know it, you are one of the millions of people who have a new gym membership, but never get to the gym more than once or twice after that initial emotional high.

Improving your nutrition and staying active are vitally important to living a truly fulfilling and healthy lifestyle, but it's not just about setting goals. If your goals are shallow, or if they don't coincide with your deeper purpose, they won't have any real value and it will become much easier for you to quit.

Instead, first determine your current vision and missions for your deep purpose. Then, tackle one or two behavior-based goals at a time. This increases your chances of not only achieving your goals, but also living out your purpose.

Once you've mastered the first one or two behavior-based goals, then start striving for the next one or two behavior-based goals on your list. *Baby steps.*

I often tell my clients, "This is not a race." If you are trying to lose weight, it may have taken you years, if not decades, to put on that weight. Even if you pace yourself, it will take you less time to lose and keep off the weight, if you're aiming for consistency rather than some unhealthy trendy diet.

Going back to Rosa – she recognized that her meaningful purpose was to be able to support her son who had special needs, along with supporting her entire family. She also recognized that teaching her children how to live a healthier, more energetic life was part of her primary purpose.

Self-discovery is crucial to uncovering a meaningful purpose that will allow you to clearly define your vision and mission.

Ask the Tough Questions

Most of the time, we don't want to ask the hard questions. It's easier to focus on the superficial concerns, especially considering how we're bombarded by superficial advertisements promising cheap, fleeting pleasures ... empty-calorie meals, looking a certain way, living a certain lifestyle, and so on.

Ask yourself why you might have been unmotivated in the past to continue changing your self-sabotaging habits to healthier ones.

Only you can answer that question. I cannot answer it for you.

I recommend that you dig deep to find the answers to these personal questions. To understand why transforming your life to a better, healthier state is important to you, you need to know your true self.

Perhaps, like Rosa, you have children who are an integral purpose in your life. If this is the case, take time to reflect on the truth that parents are role models to their children. Children learn more effectively from their parents by example, versus you simply telling your children what to do. If you have children, your habits are being mimicked by them. This can make for a truly meaningful purpose for you when it comes to pursuing your goal of changing self-sabotaging behaviors.

If you have serious health issues and your doctor has told you that something needs to change, the desire to live and continue pursuing other passions in life may be a valuable purpose. Perhaps you've reached a point where changing up your lifestyle is your only option.

Once you connect to something truly meaningful to you, that reason will help you achieve success in building new, transformational habits.

Ask yourself what resonates with you. What causes you to wake up in the middle of the night and worry, "I may not be able to ..."

- be the role model I want to be for my children.
- achieve all my career goals.
- be able to travel.
- enjoy a pain-free day.
- achieve something else.

Whatever it is, focus on that answer and begin narrowing down your focus as far as you can. The deeper you go, the more powerful that force becomes in helping you press on when change becomes work, when it takes a lot of effort and challenges you to move past your comfort zone. Because it is going to challenge you. And that is where most people stop – because they didn't connect those goals to any meaningful purpose.

"Vision is the art of seeing what is invisible to others." — Jonathan Swift

Self-Discovery: Your Vision + Mission

You may understand your goals, which might be things such as:

- Improving your food choices to more nutrient-dense foods
- Exercising to lose weight
- Building stronger muscles
- Having more energy throughout your day

That's terrific!

But *why* are these goals important to you?

Seriously.

Why?

Do your goals serve your purpose?

To answer this, you need to critically brainstorm and reflect *objectively*, not emotionally.

One of the most common denominators I find with people who set out to change their food choices and exercise routines is that these decisions have been based on emotion. Such goal-setters may have been insulted by a family member or friend, or worse, themself. Perhaps pressures from social media are wearing them down. Or perhaps they get winded climbing one flight of stairs and feel embarrassed about that.

Emotions are powerful, but when you're talking about major life changes, you need to focus on objectivity, not emotional aspects.

Also, you have to separate your needs from your wants.

There's a big difference between something you need and something you want.

A want is not a priority. A want is not a purpose. A want is not deeply meaningful. Typically, a *want* is nothing more than something which offers instant gratification or a distraction to temporarily fill a void.

Needs are priorities, connecting you with purpose and true meaning.

Write down all of the things you think you *need* to live the life you desire and to feel fulfilled. Remember to stay focused specifically on *you*. This is not what your spouse needs or what your children need. This is completely about *your* needs for achieving *your* fulfilled life.

Do not limit yourself. Simply brainstorm and write. If this takes you a couple of days, that's fine. Just take your list with you everywhere you go and jot down ideas as they come. Since most of us always have our smartphones with us, using a note application could work best.

I encourage you to allow your mind to process this question for a couple of days. Keep modifying and updating this list as your self-reflection evolves.

Then, prioritize all of your needs. When you patiently complete this process, you'll begin to recognize the things that are truly the *most* meaningful to you.

Now, prioritize your list even more to find the top five most deeply meaningful *needs* for your life. For example, this could involve raising children to become positive, integral parts of society, reaching the top position in your career field, striving to become the healthiest version of yourself to be a good role model for your family, transitioning to a different career, providing caregiving for a family member, and the list goes on.

Your purpose truly starts to become recognizable once you have uncovered what is genuinely important to you. With this list, your priorities will shift from being pointed towards a wishful, unperceivable dream to a vision that represents an achievable mission.

Raise Your Standards

"Any time you sincerely want to make a change, the first thing you must do is to raise your standards." — Anthony Robbins

Personal Standards

Most of us hear these types of sayings (or see them plastered on social media) all the time:

- "You have to raise your standards."
- "You deserve better than this."
- "You have to raise your standards to reach success."
- "Never settle."

It's awesome when you know that you deserve better than what you have – whether we're talking about a current relationship that isn't fulfilling, a job you're unhappy with, less-than-ideal living conditions, the way you look, or even the way you feel. Up to this point in time, your personal standards have allowed you to remain where you are.

This is why motivational speakers so often talk about the importance of raising your standards.

If we don't raise our standards, what do we expect? A person who remains in an abusive relationship doesn't deserve it, but they often feel like there's no other option ... no way out. They don't know their worth, so they settle.

Our personal standards can be a part of the delusion of thinking we deserve less. These have the potential to be self-sabotaging beliefs we tell ourselves. You may know someone who tends to settle for certain things in their life. Maybe you've been frustrated because they offer constant excuses for why they can't seem to change things.

- "He can change. I love him."
- "I hate my job, but it provides a steady paycheck."
- "What if I fail? I don't want to take that risk."

Those beliefs are all rooted in personal standards. Unfortunately, until standards are raised, a person will most likely remain stuck where they are.

It isn't until someone says *"Enough!"* that they begin to raise their personal standards.

Our Comfort Zone

Too often, we tend to stay with the same basic standards we've had for a long time because they're simply comfortable.

Most of us prefer things to be comfortable. When things change, that's when we get uncomfortable.

It is a natural, biological tendency. Our bodies will always try to be as comfortable as possible and return to homeostasis.

But if we want to raise our standards, to move past survival mode, we must be willing to get out of our comfort zones. And if we want to get out of our comfort zones, we must raise our standards.

The two go hand in hand, don't they?

For many of us, our comfort zones are vices. When we're stressed, worried, or overwhelmed with the daily rigors of life, we may go to the bag of chips, the bar of chocolate, the glass of wine or beer, or other personal vice.

These are the comforts – the things that help us feel like we're escaping our turbulent emotions or our rough day. In reality, these things are simply instant gratifications. They're a Band-Aid when what we need is surgery.

Unfortunately, if our current state of being is keeping us wrapped up in worry, stress, anxiety, or any other negative state, we cannot break away from it until we create cognitive awareness of it. We must understand that we *do have the power* to change this.

Awareness Empowers Transformation

The opportunity for transformation is only possible through discovering our deeper meaning. If we become aware of our comfort zone habits and the patterns of behavior that we wrap ourselves in, then we'll have the first opportunity to make the decision to raise our standards.

How?

You can certainly write goals down on paper and put your priorities on a calendar, and then take the first steps. But transformation requires more than that. Once you're connected to what's truly meaningful to you (as we have discussed), then you must decide to take action steps. That decision is the turning point for your standards.

Whatever you want to achieve in life, it truly is up to you. You have the power to do it! The first step in raising your standards is to build a stronger awareness for yourself.

Awareness empowers you.

Whatever your reality is, or has been up to this point, when you focus on improving your awareness and raising your standards, you will be empowering yourself!

Life has often been described as a progression of changing seasons. Life constantly brings us new seasons and new opportunities for change. Our priorities are constantly evolving with each passing season.

When you were a teenager, your priorities were probably hanging out with friends, going to parties, or even studying for exams so you could get into a good college.

In your 20s, those priorities likely involved to finding a good employer to build your career upon. You might have been focused on getting married and raising a family. And when you had children – whether in your 20s or 30s – they became a top priority.

You see, our priorities change and evolve as we age and move through the different seasons of our lives. Yet, we need to raise our standards in order to make the necessary changes.

Essential Steps for Raising Your Standards

First and foremost, you need to believe in yourself. This may very well be the most important first step. If you don't have faith in yourself that you can achieve your goals, then that negative voice in your head is going to stop you each and every time.

You must honestly believe that you're capable of achieving the goals you set for yourself. You may have family and friends who support you, but you'll also have naysayers, "negative Nancy's" who may not want you to succeed. You need to shut those voices out and embrace the ones who believe in you.

And the strongest voice of belief should be your own.

Second, you need to admit that you make mistakes, but not hold it against yourself. We all fall short at some point. When we keep "beating ourselves up" every time we miss the mark, fall short, or quit, we'll instinctively go back to that old comfort zone.

This only pushes you further away from your goals – not closer. You are human. It's okay. It's in these experiences where we fall short and face challenges that we discover who we truly are. And if we self-reflect, we learn how to be better next time.

Third, you need to have better awareness and control over your time. Time is precious. Some say it's the most precious commodity we have because each second that is gone is gone for good.

Everyone is busy. That's not a valid explanation for why you cannot start working towards your goals. You will always make time if it is something that is deeply meaningful to you and thus a priority. If you keeping using the excuse that "I'm too busy," let this be an opportunity for you to self-reflect on why you tell yourself and others this.

Make the best use of your time. For example, instead of watching TV, you could better spend your time preparing for the next day, exercising, doing yoga or meditation, spending quality time with your family, reading, and so on.

Fourth, you need to stand up for yourself. As I just mentioned, you will find plenty of people who don't want you to improve or change. It's like crabs in a bucket. Ever heard that expression? If you stick a bunch of crabs in a bucket, they move around. If one's trying to get out and manages to grasp the top edge of the bucket with their claw, and starts pulling himself out, the other crabs will reach up and grab him and pull him back down to the bottom.

Some people are just like those crabs stuck in the bottom of the bucket. They don't want to see you improve because, if you improve, it's only going to point out that their standards have remained too low.

Fifth, you must hold your integrity intact. Clearly define your moral code and stand your ground. When you have strong principles and raise your standards, you'll notice the conduct, thoughts, and expressions of some people to be more corrosive than you might have recognized in any past experiences.

You will have a different perspective on things. When your standards are raised, your integrity will be tested even more because many people don't set high standards for themselves. So, hold fast to your principles and you will achieve your goals.

Sixth, finally, let's discuss excuses. I briefly touched on this in the third key point. No matter what subject matter we're talking about, excuses seem to be rampant these days. Whether it's a personal or professional matter, we all know someone in our lives who typically cancels on us at the last minute or gives an excuse as to why they can't do "XYZ." Because this happens to most people quite often, our society is starting to become jaded. We must remember that there are excuses, and then there are explanations. Explanations are the genuine and honest reasoning behind a decision or action. Excuses serve as a "cover-up" justification for your decision or action.

For example, let's say you promised a friend, in advance, that you'd help them move out of their apartment. Moving day is in a couple of weeks and you don't want to help anymore, but you feel bad. The explanation would simply be, "I changed my mind, and I don't want to help anymore. I apologize. Is there someone else who can help you?" The excuse you tell your friend for why you can't do it would be a lie along the lines of, "Oh, I just remembered I have an appointment I can't miss," or "My back has been killing me."

Covering up the truth with lies seems to be more important to our society than simply being honest. We're too worried about how the other person will react, but without actually knowing how they will react – and we are losing our integrity.

Always be honest with yourself and others. Try to be more conscious of when you tend to give yourself, or others, excuses rather than the real explanation. When you raise your standards, the excuses that have been holding you back start to disappear because you're more focused more on honesty, integrity, and holding yourself accountable.

Meet Olivia

When I first met Olivia, she was a newlywed in her early 40s. She was a respectful, kind, and courteous woman – the type of woman who would basically do anything for anyone. We probably all know an Olivia. Someone who would happily give you the shirt off their back. At her core, she was empathetic and ready to help any person in need.

But she wasn't someone you could push around or take advantage of. She understood where to draw the line.

When Olivia and I had our initial meeting, she'd only been married for a short time. According to her, she and her husband both viewed this as a new chapter in their lives, a new opportunity, and a chance to avoid the mistakes they'd both made in previous relationships.

They'd talked about starting a family in the near future, but Olivia knew it wouldn't be a good idea for her – not with her current state of health. She knew that if she were to become pregnant, it could potentially create a health issue for her and possibly her baby.

You see, Olivia wasn't healthy. Over the years, she'd gained considerable weight.

She admitted she'd tried many different exercise regimens, nutrition plans, pills, and other trendy, get-fit-quick schemes, but she'd only found herself adding *more* weight.

Olivia had grown frustrated. While her health hadn't been a real concern for her in the past, her standards had now changed.

She was excited about this new chapter in life – her marriage and the prospect of starting a family. Her standards had been raised because her priorities had changed.

What had really changed, though?

Was it getting married? Was it the idea of having children? After all, plenty of women who are overweight or even obese get pregnant and have children, with no health issues for either the mom or the baby. Yes, the risk of pregnancy increases for people who are significantly overweight, but in our society, it happens over and over again.

So, for Olivia, what had really changed?

It was the new goal of wanting to have a healthy lifestyle and a healthy family. She knew that once she learned more about nutrition, exercising, how to lose weight, and how she could incorporate new healthy food choices into her routine, she could then set an example for her husband, who would then follow suit and become healthier as well. Then, she could give her children a healthy start in life.

She'd found what was deeply meaningful to her in this new marriage and recognized that her current standards were no longer good enough.

If she had come to me and said that her husband wanted her to lose weight, what do you think would have happened? She wouldn't have raised her standards for herself; she would have tried to do it only because her husband wanted her to.

Keep in mind that you can raise your standards for someone else, but that's called an external or extrinsic motivator. Research has shown time and time again that external motivation may have short-term impacts but have no positive influence long-term. In fact, such motivation can be detrimental. That kind of motivation is short-lived because you're doing what you're doing for someone else rather than for yourself.

Olivia's motivation was internal. It was intrinsic. Her first priority was to reduce her body fat percentage. The body transformation plan I put together for her focused on exercise, healthier food choices, and improving her mindset habits: Mind, body, and spirit.

Olivia's Partner in "Crime"

In the beginning of our time working together, Olivia relied on me to keep her accountable. Whenever you raise your standards and seek to pursue specific goals, having an accountability partner is critical.

Can you be successful without an accountability buddy in your life? Sure, but when you must be accountable to someone else – when you have to relay information about what you did or didn't do, what you ate, if you worked out, and so on – it helps improve your success rate for staying on track.

Olivia recognized that having me hold her accountable was one imperative key to her early success. As time progressed, she needed the "good pressure" of being accountable to me less and less because her actions became routine and automatic.

That's how it should be. In the beginning, you're going to be facing new challenges, new expectations, and new goals that are foreign to you. Your comfort zone is going to call you back constantly, and it will be difficult to ignore that call at first. That's why having an accountability partner significantly increases the chances of succeeding for most people.

After a few months, you'll most likely not need to have your accountability person holding you accountable. You'll develop the patterns, habits, routines, and rituals that then become much easier. Your comfort zone will no longer be as enticing or vocal in your mind.

After five months, Olivia had lost nearly 50 pounds. Consistency is certainly a key factor in that kind of weight loss, as is shifting to a completely healthy lifestyle, but that loss happened because Olivia raised her standards, understood what was truly and deeply meaningful to her, and put her priorities into action.

That is what helped her stay focused, determined, and tenacious.

Takeaways from Olivia

Olivia had entered a new chapter in her life. She had a new life. She was motivated, and she refused to settle on what had been "good enough" in the past.

She refused to settle, like so many people do. When people settle, this can reduce or completely shut down progress.

We can settle in many ways. We can be comfortable. That comfort zone is enticing. The familiar is a powerful pull. Then, suddenly you realize you're sitting on the couch with a bag of chips or a pint of ice cream because of a stressful day. You wonder how you let this happen in the first place. (You let it happen because it feels so good!)

We may rationalize.

- "I will take action tomorrow."
- "It's only one candy bar."
- "A little drink never hurt anyone."

We're good at rationalizing just about any behavior we take on. You may think you aren't someone who rationalizes, but we've all experienced a time where we've settled. Most of the time, settling stems from being lazy, procrastinating, or being indecisive.

Sometimes, we just want to do something easy and mindless. I totally get it. But, when watching your favorite TV series with your favorite snack becomes a daily ritual, that's when we need to recognize that it might have become an unhealthy daily habit.

Never settle.

Know your worth.

Have faith and believe in yourself.

Practice self-love.

If you don't love yourself, you're going to have a real struggle when it comes to raising your standards. If you don't love yourself, you won't really be able to raise your standards at all. Why? Because personal standards are all about love.

How do you practice self-love?

Affirmations. Believing in yourself. Always assuming the best in you, not the worst. Surrounding yourself with people who also believe in you.

When Olivia came to me for guidance, I became one of the people who believed in her.

I believe in you, too. You simply have to believe in yourself also.

Remember that when you improve yourself and work on getting healthier, the people around you will see that and benefit. Your efforts will become infectious to the people who love you the most. It may not mean that everyone in your life is suddenly going to change their unhealthy ways into healthier habits, but someone will take note and be inspired by your health journey.

Olivia's husband was inspired and her actions positively influenced him to take action.

Also, if you are on social media and you start posting about your personal changes with healthy living, people will notice. They will be inspired. Why?

Because you believed in yourself and know your worth.

You practiced self-love by choosing to raise your standards.

Self-Discovery: Self-Love

One question: What is your self-love rating?

I want you to contemplate this question.

Notice that I didn't give you a scale to rate yourself on. It's not an answer between 1 and 10 or 1 and 100. It is simply a question for you to consider, evaluate, and determine the answer for yourself.

- How much do you love yourself?
- Do you love yourself?

In case you don't think you have any real worth or value, <u>you do</u>. You absolutely, most certainly, have incredible value. I have already mentioned this a few times, and I will say it a million more times until it resonates with you.

If your initial instinct to that question was to shy away from it or ignore it because you're not sure how much you love yourself, that's the first thing you must focus on. If you don't love yourself, it will be difficult for you to raise your standards.

If you can't raise your standards, your goals and priorities will start to slip further away.

I want you to do a simple activity:

Write down all of the excuses or reasons you've not yet taken action to get healthier, focus on food choices, or become more physically active, etc.

Once you complete this list, add a column to the right to write down an idea or plan for how you can dissolve these excuses.

How can you overcome your excuses?

- An accountability partner?
- Personal reminders?
- A counselor?
- By removing a behavior that's in the way of productivity?

Whatever you think will work, write it down. This may not be your final course of action, but it will start giving you some ideas on *how* to overcome the issue, which will in turn make setting and achieving goals feel more realistic and doable. This will affect your confidence, boost your self-esteem, manifest hope, aid your optimism, and invite an opportunity for love and appreciation.

Upon successfully practicing self-love and deciding to overcome our excuses, we can then set appropriate goals for ourselves.

Part 4

Setting Goals

"A goal without a plan is just a wish." — Antoine de Saint-Exupery

What is a realistic goal?

It is practical, manageable, and obtainable based on your current mindset, time frame, skills, abilities, priorities, and available resources.

I understand that most individuals are trying to live within their family's budget while balancing the available time with priorities and goals that are truly important to them.

So, how do we get realistic with our goals?

1. Write down your behavior-based goals.

Traditional goal setting focuses on outcome-based goals. For example, wanting to lose 20 pounds, running a marathon, or fitting into your old jeans, among others. Outcome-based goals are useful, but they do have their limitations. Of course, we need to know what these goals are in order to create the proper action steps to change our behavior, but we do not want to focus on them. It is important to remember that the outcome is only a distraction.

Firstly, an outcome-based goal focuses on what you want the end result to be, without specifying how you plan to get there.

Secondly, when we concentrate solely on the goal, it may feel distant and unattainable, which can make it easier to consider giving up along the way.

Third, not all goals are entirely within our control to achieve, so it's more attainable to focus on the steps we take to help us reach our goals.

On the other hand, behavior-based goals describes a specific behavior that you are ready, willing, and able to implement consistently within a realistic time frame. For example, drinking one extra glass of water each day to improve hydration, adding an extra serving of vegetables each day, jogging three times per week to prepare for a marathon, and so forth.

Focusing on behavior-based goals allows for greater flexibility in creating action steps that suit your needs and desires. As the process evolves, you gain more control over adjusting your behaviors to align with your changing requirements.

Behavior-based goals are rooted in the present, making them feel more achievable and attainable.

For the purposes of this book, I encourage you to *identify* your outcome-based goals but shift your *focus* to your practical behavior-based goals. Writing down your behavior-based goals can be particularly helpful. When you have these goals written down and visible, they serve as constant reminders to keep you on track.

2. *K.I.S.S.*

You might have heard this acronym before.

K.I.S.S. = "Keep It Simple, Silly."

If you want to reach your full potential, simplify what your most important priorities are, outlining the action steps you need to take each day. Understanding your daily routine is *key*. Simplify your action steps as much as possible so that they can seamlessly fit into your day.

If you find that the daily goals you've set for yourself aren't realistically fitting into your 24-hour day, adjust. Break down those goals even more. For any goal to be attainable, it must be *doable*. Keeping it simple helps those behavior-based goals become doable.

This is one of the reasons why I map out daily and weekly goals for my clients. I remind them that the goal is not perfection. Progress is the name of the game.

3. Take stock of what you have in place right now to achieve your goals or help you overcome potential pitfalls. This is where you list your resources.

Let's take a moment to walk through one example to help you understand this process better.

If your current outcome-based goal is to run the New York City Marathon in five years, five years is the time frame you're giving yourself in order to achieve this goal.

Now, what's motivating you to do this? Remember, internal motivators are powerful. External motivators are not. If it's an external motivator you're focused on, that could be a pitfall, threat, or liability to you achieving the goal at hand.

What kind of information do you have about running in marathons, and specifically the New York City Marathon? For example, did you know that people apply to race in the New York City Marathon for years and still get denied? Did you also know that in order to run in this marathon, you must have a record of competing in other marathons?

That could be a pitfall. It doesn't mean you can't do it, but you have to start training hard and complete other half or full marathons before you should even consider applying for the New York City Marathon.

What about training? Are you planning to jog every day? Is that going to be enough? Have you researched the training process for what it will take to allow you to start by jogging one mile per day, all the way to 26 miles on race day?

Will you need funding or financial assets to help you achieve the goal? Take note of all your expenses. If you don't have the means to pay for everything you'll need, that could be a pitfall or a minor setback. If you have the money, it's an asset.

No matter what your outcome-based goals are, once you are certain of your internal motivation, take the time to ensure that you have all the necessary resources to accomplish that goal.

4. Determine all milestones that will allow you to reach your goals.

Any goal worth pursuing has milestones.

Most of the time, we tend to focus on the overarching goal: the long-term outcome-based goal. This is a mistake because it only distracts us and can even be counterproductive. Instead, focus on the current smaller milestones and your progress. This will promote accomplishment and success for you.

For example, if you are writing a book, you start with an idea and work through it chapter by chapter, breaking it down into pages and paragraphs. Then, you have various stages of editing, cover design, and much more. These are all milestones.

When you want to get in shape by exercising or having better nutrition, it's important you determine the milestones that are reasonable and achievable for you.

The smaller you make the milestones, the bigger the sense of accomplishment you'll achieve at a faster pace.

5. Share your goals.

Share your goals, both behavior-based and outcome-based, with other people you trust and rely on – family, friends, or another support system. This promotes "good pressure" and accountability.

Along with sharing your goals, find an accountability partner who will check in with you and expect you to keep them updated with information about how you're doing at a frequency of your choice (each day, week, month, etc.).

Many people like to try to achieve their goals silently because, if they fall back or quit all together, no one will know. This type of frame-of-mind is already setting a person up for failure. From the start, a person engaging in this behavior is showing that they don't believe in themself and is foreshadowing their own future failure. This person views accountability as a "negative" thing, not an opportunity for personal growth.

This could also be a sign that someone isn't truly ready to commit to putting in the effort it takes to achieve their goals, but only they can know that. If this is the case, it's better for a person to wait until they are ready and in the right mindset. If we force anything before we're truly ready, the process usually only ends in setbacks or quitting.

When aiming at achieving goals, we should always try to give ourselves the best opportunity for success. Sharing our goals with others will increase our likelihood for success.

6. Be willing to make adjustments.

Your ultimate goal – and the milestones you set to reach that goal – may evolve as you progress through your health journey. This is completely normal. You may have to alter some or all of your perimeters for achieving your goal: your exact goal, time frame, how you will achieve it, etc. As you progress, your goal may change. Remain flexible and willing to adjust as needed.

For example, maybe you want to start a business, but don't have the financial resources right now. Perhaps your immediate goal shouldn't be to start a business, but to set aside a certain percentage of your monthly income so that one day in the future you can pursue your business venture.

7. Successful goals should essentially hold to the SMART method. They should be:

- Specific
- Measurable
- Achievable
- Relevant
- Time-based

To make a goal *specific*, think about what you're planning as a detailed mission statement. Making your goal specific will answer all of the 'w' questions: who, what, when, where, which, and why.

Making a goal *measurable* means deciding on what metrics you will use to determine when you've achieved your goal. This makes your goal more tangible.

Brainstorm whether or not your goal is *achievable* and if you have all of the skills and tools you will need. If you don't, how will you attain the skills and tools to make your goal achievable?

Make sure your goal is *relevant* by focusing on what is deeply meaningful to you and creating the action steps that help you achieve your overarching, outcome-based goal.

Lastly, no goal is ever achievable if you don't create a time frame for yourself. A *time-based* goal will help you stay on track and stay focused.

Realistic SMART goals empower you against any external forces that may try to set you back.

Meet Melanie

Melanie was a very active woman who came to me in her late 30s. She was the mother of one child and very active in her daughter's school and her local community. She worked out quite a bit, but she also had a lot of knee problems.

The ligaments, tendons, and connective tissue around the knee take a lot of abuse, especially from repetitive actions like jogging. In Melanie's case, it got to the point where she needed surgery.

She went in for surgery and then faced several limitations. One of her significant limitations was that she couldn't put any weight on that recovering leg for several months. This frustrated her beyond measure. She was a highly active person. After just a couple of weeks sitting around and waiting for things to improve, she admitted the slow recovery was driving her crazy. She started to doubt herself. Her confidence and self-esteem levels cratered to an all-time low.

This can happen to anyone in similar circumstances; after several weeks of waiting for your body to heal so that you can go back to your regular routine, you start to question whether you'll ever be able to move like you used to.

I've known many people who've had different types of surgeries or injuries; when healing is slow, people too often try to get back to their normal routine too soon. For example, they might get up from a chair and grab their crutches, but then try to put a little weight on their healing leg or foot anyway – "just to test it out" – only to be met with searing pain.

Depending on what part of the body is healing, the healing process can be slower than we want, which tests our patience. Yes, this can be frustrating. It can also affect our self-esteem and confidence levels, which can lead to doubt.

For Melanie, slow healing led to growing frustration and impatience. She just wanted to get back to her normal activities and not have to deal with the constant pain and discomfort in her knee.

When she first reached out to me, Melanie was desperate for some type of activity – some level of physical activity. She just wanted to, "keep moving."

I began working with her, but focusing on upper body and core exercises that were workable for her. There wasn't much we could focus on with her lower body because she couldn't put any weight on her healing leg; even with her crutches, she could barely stand for longer than a minute or so. Technically, she could exercise her healthy leg in a seated position, but she worried about potentially creating muscle imbalances between her two legs over time.

So, the focus was to have her doing upper body and core exercises to keep her mind preoccupied while she was in recovery.

In the beginning, Melanie had unrealistic goals for herself to get back on her feet right away. But even if everything went well, her doctors projected it would take her three to six months before she'd be able to return to her normal activities.

At the point when we met, it had been less than two months. She still had a ways to go. And, as is the case for most people who've undergone surgery like hers, once she could finally start regaining the strength in her leg, she would have to start out slow.

At times, Melanie would slip into a mild depressive state, especially when she was inactive. When this happened, I wouldn't hear from her. Basically, she would shut down.

Regaining Momentum

Because Melanie was unable to be very active, I focused on her accountability so that we could create practical behavior-based goals and promote accomplishment. Along with her upper body and core exercises, we focused on optimal nutrition, proper portion sizes, and keeping her calories in a deficit.

Understandably, Melanie was putting on weight due to being less active. For someone focused on her physical conditioning, this was negatively affecting her mental state.

I checked in with her every day to hear how everything was going and make sure she was completing her exercises, staying on track with her nutrition, and doing okay emotionally. My daily calls helped to hold her accountable for these objectives, but also accomplished something else that was important. These calls allowed her the opportunity to talk about anything and everything that was on her mind, enabling her to release her frustrations and celebrate her successes.

Slowly, things started to improve for Melanie. She was a responsible individual who didn't want to let a professional, like me, down. Accountability truly gave her the perfect amount of positive pressure to remain consistent.

She got back into a normal routine of staying as active as possible through completing her upper body and core workouts several times per week. This was her first, behavior-based goal.

Melanie's second goal was to refocus on her nutrition habits, including proper portion sizes, mindful eating, and choosing healthy food options for each meal.

The third goal was for her to work with a physical therapist each week to help her healing leg regain mobility and strength. Melanie's non-injured leg had also lost some of its strength and stamina. So, she needed to gain its strength back as well.

These were all practical behavior-based goals. Melanie stopped gaining weight because she was more active and on an appropriate nutrition plan for her. The progress she made through all of her efforts also helped her feel more accomplished. Melanie was experiencing increased positive emotions, and her self-worth and self-love had increased significantly.

I kept checking in with her daily, which allowed her to discuss anything with me: action steps, setbacks, emotions, physical responses, mindset, etc.

Five months after her surgery, Melanie was back to doing the activities she loved, and she was able to maintain laser-focus on her fitness, nutrition, and family. It was a wonderful gift for me to be able to experience and witness this kind of recovery, as well as to be a part of her health journey.

Takeaways from Melanie

The first lesson here, and perhaps the most important one, is that we must not focus on trying to "conquer the world" in one day. Something I continue to remind my clients is this: "It's not a race."

For many of us, it has taken years, if not decades, for our health to evolve (or devolve) to where it is today. But, the miracle of how quickly our bodies can adapt to a new, healthy lifestyle is astonishing! Essentially, weight that has taken years to acquire can take only months to lose! But if you tell yourself that you must lose all of your unhealthy weight *now*, right away and all at once, you only create unrealistic expectations and set yourself up to fall short. The process of creating new, healthy habits should always be one which is centered on self-love and self-care.

There is another phrase that encapsulates this: "Baby steps."

Baby steps are the way to go. Create the big, all-encompassing, huge goals you want to achieve. Then, break them down into smaller milestones, each separate milestone being something measurable and achievable that shows you are making progress on a regular basis. These realistic, short-term goals will create more opportunities for success, make your long-term goals manageable, and help keep you motivated and engaged.

Big, drastic, dramatic goals are often not sustainable. Smaller, "bite-sized" ones *are* sustainable.

Also, be willing to allow your goals to evolve with each achievement and milestone. Melanie became depressed and frustrated because she wanted to get back on her feet and do the same activities she'd enjoyed prior to surgery. That was certainly not realistic at that time.

It is critically important for anyone who undergoes surgery, or has an injury, to give themselves the proper healing time such an experience requires. If you don't allow your body to heal, and don't integrate activity back in slowly, you run a greater risk of experiencing another injury or promoting recurring injuries. This will only extend your recovery time that much longer ... which also extends your frustration, lowered self-esteem, lack of confidence, and much more.

I had to help Melanie step back and focus on smaller goals – more immediate things and milestones that she could achieve. When she was able to step back, evaluate the situation, and be held accountable for these smaller goals, she was then able to achieve them, which helped boost her self-esteem and lead to greater personal growth.

Self-Discovery: Your Short + Long-Term Goals

Are you a born leader? This may seem like an odd question when we're talking about goals, but it is pertinent. Very few people are naturally born leaders. Generally speaking, leaders must be forged and created over time. One of the biggest common denominators of the best leaders is their ability to set realistic and measurable goals for themselves and their businesses.

You might not think of yourself as a leader, but once you understand how to set realistic goals and break them down into milestones, you're preparing yourself to create success.

Believe this: You are amazing, and you are ready.

Now, for a short activity.

Based on the goals you wrote down for your Self-Discovery activity in *Part 1: Ready? Set. Goals!*, now take the time to determine which ones you would consider short-term goals and which ones would you consider long-term goals.

For your long-term goals, create smaller milestones. You can do this by understanding how long it will take you to realistically achieve your long-term goals (Example: one year). Then, work backwards, breaking down each milestone by a specific frequency (Example: each month, week, etc.).

In the "Feel Good Again Workbook," download available for free on my website, page 17 features a guide to assist you in organizing this process. The link to this free workbook download is listed on page 1 in this book.

Each of these milestones will work toward a specific goal. Do this until you find yourself at the starting point of your long-term goal (Example: Day 1). This allows you to keep your overarching outcome-based goal in mind but put your daily focus on your smaller behavior-based milestones, or *the process*. **Focusing on the outcome is only a distraction.**

Be Realistic

"Realistic expectations for life are that we are going to be better today than we were yesterday, be better tomorrow than we were today. That's a plan for success." — *Jim Harbaugh*

When creating *realistic* goals for ourselves, we should aim for practical objectives that enable us to achieve success and experience a sense of accomplishment. If we set *unrealistic* goals, it only leads us to opportunities for falling short.

When discovering and setting your goals, take into consideration your lifestyle, current responsibilities, sleep-wake cycle, and where your free time exists, as well as what things in your life can be replaced with success-driven action steps, and so forth. Be honest with yourself.

One reason people don't achieve their goals is because the goals are either too easy or entirely unachievable — so, it is essential that you find a balance.

When you establish realistic goals, you empower yourself to be able to achieve them, no matter what obstacles occur.

But, let me tell you, as amazing as you are, neither you nor anyone else can control other people or outside forces. There will always be external forces trying to test or challenge you. Be prepared for this any time you're working to improve something in your life. You're bound to hit a "speedbump" at some point in your journey. The question is, will you hit it hard and potentially bottom out, or slowly cruise over it and keep going?

It is always best to set smaller, more realistic goals that are achievable, rather than to set aggressive goals that are impossible to complete based on other responsibilities which already require most of your time.

This is extremely important because giving yourself a "fighting chance" is an act of self-love that itself breeds success.

Practical + Precise

In order to provide yourself with an opportunity for success, consider reviewing several aspects of your goals to make sure they are practical and precise.

First, ask yourself: Are you practical and precise when it comes to maintaining rational and realistic mental focus? Rational thinking is important when setting goals. If you create goals based off of irrational or emotional thinking, your priorities won't be based off of what's truly meaningful to you, but rather thoughts, emotions, and 'wants' that are fleeting. In line with this, examine whether your priorities, specifically as related to your goals, are practical and precise enough to help you reach your goals. Keep in mind that your priorities and your goals are different. Your *priorities* are the things that hold great significance to you and often encompass daily responsibilities. Your *goals* are the desired outcomes you are working towards, which may or may not involve responsibilities. They might be more focused on your desires and contribute to a fulfilling life. Know that if you are practical and precise with how you intend to achieve your goals, your chances of success increase significantly.

Second, ask yourself: Are you practical and precise when it comes to acknowledging your capabilities? If you are not capable of working towards your goals because of physical, mental, or intellectual limitations, that's something you must consider. Your capabilities can be limiting, but there are ways to overcome them through research, education, personal or professional assistance, and so forth. Similarly, do you possess the practical and precise skills necessary to work through your goals? If your skills are limiting you, the same options for overcoming that problem apply.

Third, ask yourself: Are you being practical and precise in considering your available resources and allotted time frame? These aspects of setting realistic goals are incredibly important. Do you know exactly what resources you need? Are these resources available to you? If not, can you attain access to the proper resources? And, once you have the resources, are you allowing enough time to realistically accomplish your goals? This is important to determining the amount of time you'll need for success, taking into consideration for potential setbacks.

Once you consider all aspects of your goal's practicality and preciseness, you will be able to refine what your goal is to ensure it is absolutely realistic.

Measurable + Manageable

Realistic goals are also measurable and manageable. To decipher whether your goals meet these criteria, take a moment to review these aspects of your goals.

First, how do you measure and manage your goals? In other words, can you objectively observe, employ analytical thinking, and maintain flexibility to measure and manage the progress of your goals through your action steps? For example, how will you determine if you are making progress? How can you confirm whether you are losing weight at a healthy rate given your age and personal circumstances? How can you measure if the rate of my progress aligns with the time frame you've set for yourself? Once you have answered specific questions related to your goals, which allow you to measure your progress, you can then manage your goals and make any necessary adjustments.

Second, can you effectively measure and manage whether your capabilities are sufficiently facilitating progress? If you find that progress is not being achieved, there are ways to overcome this through finding completed research, seeking education, seeking personal or professional assistance, and so forth. For instance, if you have experience in building muscle effectively through strength training, you will also need to outline your plan for managing progress through periodic increases in weights, timing, tempo, and/or repetitions. These are ways you can measure whether your capabilities are adequate for generating progress.

Third, are your resources and time frame measurable and manageable? Depending on what resources you will need to complete your goals, you will need to maintain access to your resources and manage them for the entirety of your process. For example, if your fitness goal involves needing access to a gym and all of the equipment inside, a gym membership will need to fit within your budget at least until you achieve that fitness goal. Your time frame is one way you are measuring your realistic goals. Things may come up, so allowing for flexibility in your schedule is what makes your time frame manageable. You may experience setbacks like going on vacation or getting sick, or you may find out that you are achieving progress faster than you'd anticipated, which would be fantastic! Goals with rigid, predetermined expectations are not realistic.

Once you consider all aspects of your goal's measurability and manageability, your goal becomes realistic.

Obtainable

In order to provide yourself with the best possible opportunity for success, make sure your goals are actually obtainable. If a goal is obtainable, it's realistic. This is common knowledge, but let's explore the aspects that make goals obtainable as a refresher.

First, are your goals obtainable with your current mindset and priorities? In order to obtain your goals effectively, and as efficiently as possible, your mindset should be constantly laser-focused. The moment you start rationalizing why it's okay to veer off-course, that's the moment when your goal will start to become less obtainable — or at the very least, your progress will slow.

Your goals become more obtainable simply by having a systematic process involving action steps and short-term goals. If you can keep reaching your mini-milestones, your progress will continue until your goals are obtained.

Second, as mentioned before, you may not currently possess the capabilities necessary to obtain the goals that are important to you. We've already examined the resources at your disposal, which can help you understand how you might improve your capabilities. Now, it's time to take advantage of resources such as finding completed research, seeking education, pursuing personal or professional assistance to enhance any personal capabilities that may require improvement, enabling you to work toward your goals. Proactively educating yourself to improve your capabilities might require something as simple as research via the internet, articles, a book on the subject matter, informative videos, etc. You may need guidance from a mentor, but that could be someone you know who's already achieved the same goal you're striving for or contacting a professional who has expert knowledge. There are many ways to acquire the proper capabilities that will allow you to obtain your goals. The options that will work best for you will depend on what your goal is, what you still need to know, and do.

Third, are your resources and time frame obtainable? By establishing whether or not your resources are practical, we've essentially discovered whether they are obtainable, as well. If it's practical, it's most likely obtainable. But, if not, consider how you will gain access to the resources you need in order to make your goals obtainable. Do these resources originate from a media source, a family member or friend, or a co-worker, or are you able to seek out your resources independently? Are your resources free or do they entail an additional expense? Are they local, or do you need to travel to acquire them? These are some questions I would suggest you self-reflect on.

Lastly, have you created a time frame that's realistic enough to allow you to obtain your goals? No matter what time frame you have given yourself, the good news is that if your deadline is not set around a specific date or event, you can always adjust it. As your progress evolves, so may your time frame.

Diving deep into these details will allow you to successfully create realistic goals for yourself, but there's still another critical element to helping you stay on track with your goals.

Be Accountable

"Accountability is the glue that ties commitment to the result.
— Bob Proctor

We've already touched on this lightly, but let's go a little deeper.

Owning a car is a luxury. We may not know much about how it works, but we know when we sit behind the steering wheel, start it up, put it in drive, and press on the gas pedal, that it moves. There are many parts *critical* to that car being able to move on its own, but that doesn't mean we understand them.

In many ways, success is like this. Remove one critical component, and you may have some success for a little while, but eventually the entire "engine" of your life, and the goals you've set for yourself, will seize up and stop working.

Accountability is one of those critical components that helps create success in life. It fuels success. It's not always easy to implement, and, to be honest, a lot of people try to avoid accountability entirely when it comes to goal-setting. After all, if no one knows you're trying to put effort into reaching new goals, you won't have to worry about them discovering that you've quit.

Yet, if you don't have someone holding you accountable and don't have some measure of accountability in your life, the odds of you quitting increase dramatically.

This may seem very simple and straightforward. Just ask someone you trust to hold you accountable. Sounds reasonable, right? Yet, there are many challenges when it comes to accountability ... especially when you turn to your loved ones.

For example, your spouse or partner is someone you count on and should be able to rely on. Someone whom you've turned to countless times for their opinion and advice. This is the person who you love perhaps more than life itself.

They'd make the perfect accountability partner, wouldn't they?

Maybe.

But, here's the issue: What happens when they try to keep you accountable by asking you for a rundown of the things you did or didn't do on a particular day? If you had a bad day, feel frustrated, or fell short, you may answer this question emotionally.

Most likely, this could be the outcome. After all, it's the people we love the most who become the easiest targets for our frustration. Before long, that "accountability partner" is no longer going to want the job.

Accountability is not about trying to catch another person when they are "failing" – that's not at all what accountability is.

Instead, accountability is simply a reference to the effort required when it comes to holding someone to a specific set of goals and promoting success by means of positive pressure.

The opposite of your partner being the ideal option is also possible: While a family member or close friend could be a great option, what if they're typically your enabler? Secretly, for selfish reasons, they may not hold you accountable at all. For example, if you're trying to stop drinking alcohol, maybe *they* actually want to go somewhere for a social drink, so they're always telling you, "It's just one drink." Or maybe you're trying to eat healthy, and they always want to get take-out for dinner. This accountability partner should be fired! There are many reasons why someone you're close to may not have your best interests in mind. Just be mindful of that.

Accountability needs to be balanced. You need to find an accountability partner who understands your goals, believes in you, supports you, and has at least some vested interest in your success. It should be someone you trust.

I have been an accountability partner to many of my clients over the years. After all, when they succeed, I succeed. It's not always easy, but a partnership like this is often critical to success. When people try to create changes in their life, the risk of quitting increases exponentially if they don't have someone to help them on their new journey.

The Benefits of Being Accountable

There are many benefits of having an accountability partner. First, it builds trust. Not only will this person trust you as you move closer and closer to your goals, but you will learn to trust them more, too.

After all, if you are counting on someone to check in with you, that forces both parties to be honest. Seeing that someone is taking time out of their day to help you achieve your goals is a good feeling, and you'll begin to realize how much they care. This is potentially a bonding experience, especially if you're each working towards certain personal goals together!

Second, it helps you improve performance. When you know someone is cheering you on and counting on you, your performance will tend to improve – as opposed to going to the gym and working out by yourself without any accountability.

It's like having that person spotting you on the free weights, watching you squat 155 pounds, pushing and straining for that last rep, and them telling you what a great job you're doing ... and then pushing you to do just one more ... and then just ONE MORE after that! Always there to help you and keep you safe, but pushing you to your max.

Third, having such a partner leads to better results. Throughout the years, I have seen that when a person seeks to improve their nutrition, exercise more, or reach any other particular goal, the results are always better if they have a genuinely invested accountability partner.

Not just sometimes. *Always.*

Now, let's get to know Tracy.

Meet Tracy

I was blessed to meet Tracy when she was in her early 50s. She was a mother of two late-teenage boys, and things had been hectic in her life between raising children and working a full-time job. Her age was quickly catching up with her.

Basically, she had gained a little weight over the years.

Tracy had a predominantly sedentary lifestyle and always found herself lacking energy and feeling lazy after a stressful day at work.

She knew she hadn't been living a healthy life. Eventually, that could lead to more serious health issues as she cruised through those 50s and into her 60s, and she wanted to stay healthy long-term.

Her goals were to lose weight and run a half-marathon in five months. This was quite ambitious, especially considering her sedentary lifestyle. She went for a few walks each week with one of her sons, and she was trying to work her way up to jogging more.

Tracy used to do yoga, and she'd loved it, but for reasons she never admitted to me, she'd let it go and never returned to it.

Life can do that to you. You love doing something, but end up setting it aside for whatever reason, and then before you realize it, many months have passed and you still haven't gone back to it. And it becomes that much more difficult to return to healthy exercise habits when you've grown comfortable plopping down on the couch after a long day at work.

While she had ambitious goals, her deeply meaningful purpose for losing weight and exercising was because she wanted to be around for her boys when they grew older. She wanted to have more energy, too, and knew that healthier eating habits and exercise would give her the energy she was missing.

She also recognized that her boys were at that age where they'd be looking to her for how to cook and prepare meals. She hoped they'd learn how to eat healthier for when they went off and lived on their own, so her second goal was to work on cooking healthier meals that didn't take a long time to prepare.

Tracy didn't have a gym membership, so she was focusing on her outside walks before meeting me. She tried several times to push herself a little more than with simple walking. She'd try jogging but tired too easily and would quickly return to walking. She'd do several days of walking/jogging, but when her muscles ached or she didn't feel like running, she skipped a day. This became a pattern.

Tracy knew she needed accountability.

As I talked to Tracy and listened to her story, I recognized she was great at forming excuses. She would rationalize why she did or didn't need to do something. That's why family or friends weren't going to be optimal options for her when it came to serving as her accountability partner. She would just push back until they gave up.

If she didn't have accountability, Tracy was never going to reach her goal of running a half-marathon. It simply wasn't realistic.

Set up a Schedule

Together, we worked on a schedule for exercise. I wanted her to start out slowly so she wouldn't tire out her muscles to the point of feeling like she had to take a day off when she was supposed to be exercising. That said, I created a progressive schedule so she'd be challenging her body a little more each week. We established accountability check-ins to keep her on track.

When a person like Tracy is trying to make habit changes, regular accountability check-ins are imperative. In the beginning, daily check-ins are best.

Tracy also wanted guidance to understand if she was making the right choices, at least until she grew confident enough to make those decisions for herself.

Progress, Not Perfection

Tracy and I worked out a nutrition plan that focused on progress, not perfection. One of the biggest mistakes too many of us make when pursuing goals of fitness, improved nutrition, and an overall healthier lifestyle is that we tend to look for perfection. And, if we fall short (which we will because no one is perfect), that shortcoming leads to frustration and we inevitably quit.

Frustration can lead to doubt, and doubt is one of the enemies of progress. As with anything in life, nothing is perfect. So, why are we trying to accomplish the impossible?

Instead of going for perfection, I helped Tracy focus on progress. Initially, instead of having her focus on "perfect" food choices, we focused on simple, quick dinner recipes that didn't require her to expend a lot of energy on cooking after a long and tiring day at work.

I also created a progressive training program to help prepare her for the half marathon. Over time, her training progressed; her weekly runs consisted of longer "distance" days, short "sprint" days, easy-does-it jog days with medium distance, and, of course, rest days.

Together, we agreed that she should *not* go straight to the couch once she got home from work. Every time she did this, she understandably lost motivation to do anything else; she grew tired because she was comfortable. Instead of her collapsing onto the couch, I encouraged her to go for a walk, do some yoga, or take advantage of her in-home treadmill.

This immediately kicked off weight loss. She was excited to feel the absence of the weight she shed each week. In the beginning, it was tough for her – not only when it came to Tracy keeping to her training schedule along with the rest of her busy life, but also learning a different way to make healthier dinners for her family. But it didn't take long for her to find her groove and for everything to become routine. Her sons even started helping with dinner.

As she got closer to her race day, her nutrition started to shift. Her carbohydrates consumption significantly increased, with fat and fiber being reduced. The couple of days before her race, and the day itself, were extremely important. We "dialed her in" ... and the result was that she had more energy during her run than she'd ever had before!

I got a call right after she finished the half marathon, and the excitement in her voice was as clear as day. I couldn't have been prouder and happier for her and her results. It was such a blessing to be a part of that journey with her.

Takeaways from Tracy

Hopefully, by now, you understand that accountability is imperative to success. It was critical for Tracy's success, as it has been for most of the clients I've worked with.

Most people need some type of accountability, especially when they're at the early stages of building new, healthy habits. The issue is that many people try to change their lifestyle on their own.

But it all starts in the mind and with belief in yourself. If you do not have that foundation, reaching your goals may become even more difficult to accomplish.

If you truly want to succeed, though, like Tracy did, there is power in accountability. Having accountability and a support system offers encouragement, hope, and an opportunity. Sure, at times, you may become frustrated with your accountability partner, but that's really a redirection of feeling disappointment with yourself.

This is why you need someone who'll be there with you through the highs and lows. You need someone who will understand, especially in the beginning, that there will be times of extreme frustration and missed opportunities.

At some point, most of us fall short – especially in the beginning. There will be days when you don't reach your goals for the day.

Do not worry.

Understand that without accountability, it's much easier for you to lean on excuses and rationalize another day away when you fall short of your expectations.

Creating new habits is hard, and it takes time. This is when accountability should come into play and provide you the best opportunity for success.

Self-Discovery: Are You Accountable?

To be successful, you need to understand your accountability needs. Everyone is different. While Tracy recognized she needed someone to hold her accountable, you may need different tools for accountability.

In the beginning, to help you stay accountable, I highly recommend having a person to remain accountable to, rather than just a smartphone application or blank calendar for tracking. Once you've adapted to your new healthy habits and you've figured out what works best for you, then feel free to use other resources.

I also highly recommend that you announce your goals to anyone within your support system. Text them, call them, send out an email, or post to your social media accounts! Let everyone know what you're planning to do. Not only will this inspire others to look at their own lives and maybe seek out change, too, but they will start consistently following your success.

As your transformation begins, your true friends and the people who care the most about you will emerge. Likewise, the ones who are not true friends will show their "ugly faces" by being unsupportive. Keep your focus and ignore the naysayers. Unfortunately, there are people out there who will despise you when they see you changing your life for the better. Use their doubt to fuel your progress, and free yourself from their negative energy.

You don't need it. You are strong and unstoppable!

Your Support System

Your support system should be made up of people you trust and count on – those who can offer encouragement. There are going to be times when you fall short and miss the mark. Your confidence may decrease, and you may want to give up. This is normal.

Your support system should include people you can turn to and count on to help encourage you, lift you up, and get you out of any negative mindset and back to being motivated and driven, so that you can keep working toward your goals.

This support system should be made up of people who will truly be there for you during every step of your journey. For example, these could be people that know and love you, or it could be a community of like-minded individuals working toward the same goals. Regardless, choose them wisely.

Hold Yourself Accountable

Have a designated place where you write down all of your goals and milestones. Mark off each day on a calendar, journal, or diary. The things you keep track of will depend on what your goals are. If it aligns with your health goals, here are some things you could keep track of:

- Exercises you do and how you do them
- Your current body composition metrics
- Your food choices and if you're staying on track
- How you're managing stress
- Your water consumption

- Setting aside adequate recovery time

This list will be somewhat different for everyone but keep track of your main priorities and the frequencies with which you're working on them each week, or even each day.

Celebrate the milestones and accomplishments.

A few weeks from now, when you feel like nothing is improving or you're not making progress, you can look at that calendar, journal, or diary, and see proof that you are, in fact, progressing.

Tell your support system about those accomplishments, too! Smile. *Celebrate*. Allow yourself the space to be proud of yourself! Post accomplishments to social media, too. Remember, your connections on social media are following your success. You are inspiring them to make healthy changes in their lives, as well!

So, do not hide your accomplishments. Do not feel awkward about sharing the details and celebrating, either. People always love a good success story!

Now, <u>ask yourself what your accountability style is and how you would like to be held accountable.</u> Would you prefer to call your accountability partner or text them images of your completed workouts or healthy meals eaten? Would you work better by sending a video message or chatting with them in person? How about outlining all of the details of what you're doing each day or each week?

The options are endless! *What do YOU need to stay accountable to yourself and your partner?* For example, I had a client who wanted to go to a 5 A.M. group fitness class Monday through Friday. She asked if I could call her each day during the week and wake her up at 4 A.M., so that's what I did.

Identify ways that you can be successful or ways that have helped you in the past. Write down all of the things you have done in the past to be successful ... with your health, career, raising children, dealing with conflict, saving money, working hard to save up for the vacation you always wanted, or anything else.

Write down all of the different things that helped you achieve success. These are some things that work for me:

- Announcing to my Husband the goals I will be focusing on
- Setting different alerts on my smartphone
- Putting Post-it reminders all over my desk
- Keeping to-do lists, both physical and digital
- Announcing my new health goals on social media for accountability and to inspire
- Keeping track of everything I am doing in my smartphone calendar

Once you have your list, analyze the top three methods that work for you and gear them toward your new goals. If you know something that has worked for you, there's no sense in trying to reinvent the wheel.

Part 5

The Secrets to Your Full Potential

"The will to win, the desire to succeed, the urge to reach your full potential ... these are the keys that will unlock the door to personal excellence." — Confucius

What does it truly mean to achieve your *full potential?* It's a phrase many of us use, sometimes more regularly than we realize, but the depth of its true meaning often eludes us.

You might find yourself building a great career, raising healthy children, living in an idyllic neighborhood, and cultivating meaningful friendships. You may have a loving family, and everything you could ever have hoped for, but does that necessarily mean you've unequivocally reached and achieved your full potential?

Possibly.

Yet, for most people, there lingers a sense of unfinished business. After all, aren't we all still a work in progress?

Consider those moments when you find yourself amidst a Sunday evening, wondering where the week went or feeling as though time is slipping away from you. What does it signify? It's likely an indication of busyness, but could it also imply that you perhaps weren't able to accomplish all you had hoped or needed to? In such instances, you might not have fully realized your potential, especially in the context of living your healthiest life.

There are five key components that are often overlooked when it comes to achieving full potential in the realm of living a healthy lifestyle. While many of us contemplate working out and eating healthier, do we genuinely consider choosing to get more sleep, investing time in managing our stress levels, prioritizing improved hydration, or consciously focusing on our mood and how we navigate our day—both with ourselves and with others?

Probably not.

Yet, attaining all of these collectively is how we reach our full potential with our personal health.

The real measure of reaching your full potential isn't just about hitting external milestones. It's about finding a good balance within yourself and taking care of your well-being. Think of it like an ongoing journey to understand yourself better, like an adventure that encourages you to discover not only the highs of achievement but also the core of who you truly are. This journey pushes you toward a life that aligns with your most genuine self.

Meet Lexi

Lexi was a very active, fit woman in her late 40s when we met. To most people on the outside, she appeared to have everything going for her and working in her favor. She worked out five to six days a week and never made excuses. Her priority was living a healthy lifestyle for herself and her family – every single day.

She was so in tune with her exercise and nutritional routines that they were second nature. That’s a goal we all aspire to achieve!

Lexi was also a no-nonsense person who understood her self-worth. She practiced self-love, was confident without being arrogant, and wouldn't settle for anything less than what she desired out of life.

She understood that every day was a blessing and was absolutely the epitome of a lover of life.

But where she was at this point was not where she'd been throughout most of her adult life. In fact, over the years, she had successfully shed over a hundred pounds simply by exercising regularly and eating healthy. Yet, she wanted to lose more weight. She felt as though she had hit a plateau and had been lingering at her current body fat percentage.

This pause in her progress was beginning to create frustration and stress for her. She tried progressing her exercise routines by pushing a little harder, and yet nothing improved.

A quick note: short-term plateauing can occur. You're going to face peaks and valleys as well as plateaus in your progress. If you experience a week or two without progress, give yourself more time. One to two weeks is not long enough to be considered a serious plateau. Yet, when you experience a long-term plateau, that generally means something in your routine needs to be reviewed and modified.

Even though Lexi had become incredibly successful with her exercise routines and food choices, she was overlooking other important factors that most people simply don't consider, especially for women. There are other less obvious factors that we need to keep in mind when striving for optimal health.

When I sat down with Lexi, we looked at these five aspects:

1. Stress Management
2. Proper Recovery
3. Sleep Quality

4. Hydration
5. Hormone Levels

Let’s explore these now.

Stress Hormone Management

"Sometimes the most productive thing you can do is relax."
— Mark Black

Every single one of us deals with stress. You cannot escape it. The only thing you can do is manage it by working through it in order to alleviate some of the pressure.

There are several hormones that play a role in the body's response to stress. These hormones work together to coordinate that response, helping to activate energy and prepare for a perceived threat. It is important to remember that the stress response is a complex physiological process involving the interaction of multiple hormones and systems in the body. Some of the key stress hormones include:

- Cortisol: Often referred to as the primary stress hormone, cortisol is released by the adrenal glands in response to stress.
- Epinephrine (Adrenaline): Released by the adrenal glands, epinephrine is responsible for the "fight or flight" response in stressful situations.
- Norepinephrine: This hormone works alongside epinephrine to increase heart rate and prepare the body for action during stress.
- Adrenocorticotropic Hormone (ACTH): Released by the pituitary gland, ACTH stimulates the adrenal glands to produce cortisol in response to stress.
- Oxytocin: Often referred to as the "bonding hormone," oxytocin is released during stress to promote social bonding and support.

There are many different kinds of stressors that can activate our stress hormones. A stressor is something that disrupts our body's homeostasis. A stress-inducing factor triggers our sympathetic nervous system, our "fight-or-flight" response, allowing us to react to and manage any harm inflicted on the body while restoring equilibrium as swiftly as possible. Stressors can originate externally from actual sources or be brought up internally based on our personal perceptions or imaginations.

Physical Stressors

- Alcohol, drugs, and medications
- Being pregnant or breastfeeding
- Exercise
- Illness and disease
- Inadequate dietary habits
- Injury
- Insufficient or low-quality sleep
- Microorganisms (viruses, bacteria, parasites, etc.)
- Reduced caloric intake or fasting
- Time zone disruption (jet lag)
- Tobacco use

Mental Stressors

- Anxiety, worry, or negative thoughts
- Decision-based mental exhaustion
- Excessive cognitive demands (multitasking)
- Information overload
- Mental health conditions

- Mindset and mental ability challenges
- Navigating tasks in a non-native language
- Striving for perfection

Emotional Stressors

- Embarrassment and remorse
- Fear and unease
- Hostility and aggression
- Solitude, seclusion, and/or detachment from others
- Sorrow, bereavement, sadness, and/or depression

Existential Stressors

- Concerns about one's role or significance in the world
- Experiencing depression or profound sadness
- Feelings of hopelessness or apathy
- Lack of meaning or purpose
- Loss of assurance or belief system

Relational or Social Stressors

- Absence of "belonging" or community
- Cultural shock (moving to a new country or region)
- Feelings of solitude or seclusion
- Limited social standing or prestige
- Social rejection or criticism from others
- Unhealthy or dysfunctional relationships; interpersonal strife

Environmental Stressors

- Acts of violence
- Disorder
- Disturbances of the natural light-dark cycles
- Extreme circumstances (heat or cold; high altitudes)
- Loud noises and unpleasant smells
- Pollution and toxins

Stress is an unavoidable part of our lives, manifesting in various forms and arising from a multitude of sources, as outlined above in the categories of physical, mental, emotional, existential, relational, and environmental stressors.

Understanding the nature of stress and its impact on our body's equilibrium is essential. By recognizing stressors and actively working to manage them, we can alleviate some of the pressure imposed on us.

It is crucial to realize that stress management is not only about physical well-being but also the preservation of our mental and emotional health.

By taking proactive steps to address and cope with stress, we can lead healthier, more balanced lives and achieve a greater sense of overall personal well-being.

Our stress response always follows this pattern:

1. Start off in a dynamic equilibrium
2. Encounter a stressor
3. Respond to the stressor
4. Recover and rebuild

5. Enter a new homeostasis/baseline

Unfavorable patterns of behavior frequently arise as coping mechanisms for stress, anxiety, trauma, intense emotions, and challenging situations. Unhealthy habits should not be dismissed as arbitrary decisions or indications of laziness, a lack of motivation, or self-destructiveness. Every behavior (positive or negative) stems from an effort to address a problem or challenge.

Positive stressors are short-lived, infrequent, over in a matter of minutes or hours, and can become a positive experience.

Negative stressors last a long time, are chronic, ongoing, depressing, unmotivating, and/or stressors which break us down to a worse state than we were in before.

Let's not forget that, when we're stressed, our bodies release cortisol, which is a hormone produced by the adrenal glands. Cortisol serves an important purpose in helping us deal with stress by regulating various functions in the body.

When it comes to weight loss, cortisol can have some effects that might make it a bit more challenging to lose weight, though. Our stress response is managed in our bodies through hormones, and it can change our entire hormonal makeup. Cortisol impacts our metabolisms, as this hormone increases glucose levels in the bloodstream and spikes the secretion of insulin. High amounts of insulin create fat storage. Elevated cortisol levels over a long period of time can contribute to weight gain, particularly around the midsection. Such levels can increase our cravings for unhealthy, high-calorie foods, which can derail our weight loss efforts.

Many times, I have heard someone mention how they experienced a stressful time in their life and correlated that stress to losing weight. But this is an inaccurate analysis. Cortisol can potentially make it difficult for someone to lose weight, but there are other factors that happen in a stressful circumstance which can result in weight loss. When you are stressed, this is often indicative of a busy time in your life. And when you're busy, you're typically more active; extremely busy individuals tend to not consume as many calories because they're forgetting to eat or skipping meals.

But here's the thing: Cortisol is just a small piece of the puzzle. Losing weight involves a combination of factors, including calorie intake, physical activity, and individual metabolism. While cortisol can potentially make weight loss a bit trickier, it doesn't mean losing weight is impossible.

First, though, it's good to know what you're dealing with. Here are five ways stress can make losing weight more difficult:

Precisionnutrition.com[33]

There are many rituals and methods people use to effectively manage their stress. Some people go for walks. Some people listen to music. Some people take a hot bath, meditate, do yoga, pray, go for drives, or engage in a million other things that work for them.

Develop your own stress management techniques that work best for you. Do something that calms you, clears your mind, and refocuses your energy in a positive way. The only way to know what the best option for you is, will come from experimenting.

When it came to stress management, what were Lexi's stressors, and was she proactively managing them?

It turned out that Lexi was managing her stress relatively well. She had a number of personal daily habits that helped her manage stress. These were things like:

- Staying organized and being decisive
- Creating boundaries in her life and knowing when to say "No"
- Setting aside time for herself, which created balance in her hectic life
- Sharing the "wheel of control" with other members of her family, so she wasn't burdened by herself with all of the daily duties and responsibilities

I encourage you, right now, to write down options that have worked for you in the past or that you think might work. It's always a great idea to have this list handy in case you find yourself having a stressful day or moment. Revert back to it and make use of one of your options if you feel like you could use a little relief.

Remember, a positive or negative stressor is differentiated by how well we are able to recover from the stressor.

Self-Discovery: Do You Handle Stress Well?

Are you losing your temper too easily? Are you drinking more than usual? Are you feeling tense and impatient?

It's entirely normal to experience some days that are better than others. However, it's also essential to pay attention to your emotional well-being and periodically check in with your feelings every few weeks to maintain optimal mental and emotional health. Self-awareness plays a critical role in ensuring overall well-being.

To promote this, take the stress test created by *The Guardian.*[34] These 13 questions may assess how effectively you're managing your stress. This quiz is designed to be a self-awareness tool; not a diagnostic tool.

Answer the following statements about your feelings over *the last two weeks*. Use the corresponding answers (a, b, or c) that best describes your current experience.

a. Never
b. Sometimes
c. Most of the Time

1. My mood has been a bit "down in the dumps." I've felt low, somewhat "blah," depressed, as though a fog or black cloud has been weighing me down.
2. I've lost interest in my activities, hobbies, and daily routines.
3. I can't muster the motivation to do much or engage with anyone, including people I usually enjoy spending time with.
4. I find it challenging to rest, relax, or recharge my batteries.

5. I feel tired, my quality of sleep is poor (struggling to fall asleep, waking up during the night, oversleeping) and I generally feel fatigued with minimal energy.
6. My appetite has changed. I either don't feel hungry and can't eat much, or I experience the opposite, where I can't stop eating and constantly crave certain foods.
7. I'm burdened by a persistent sense of worry, a feeling of impending dread, as if something bad is about to happen, even though I can't pinpoint it. It feels irrational, but I can't shake the feeling off or control my worrying thoughts.
8. I'm more irritable, short-tempered, and restless than usual.
9. Concentration is difficult, and even simple tasks like focusing on a TV program or reading a book prove challenging.
10. I've been experiencing some or all of these physical discomforts such as aches and pains, chest tightness or flutters, changes in bowel habits, mental fog, dizziness, feeling overwhelmed, neck pain, and headaches.
11. I've increased my alcohol consumption and/or turned to substances (including prescription medication and illegal drugs), to help me relax, cope, or escape.
12. Despite having many people around me, I feel lonely.
13. I wish everything could just "stop" for a while. I'd like to take a break for a bit to breathe and catch up with myself.

Mostly A: Feeling Good

Whatever you're doing, keep doing it. Life is ticking along nicely, and you're in a good place, so well done for putting yourself first and keeping your mental and emotional wellbeing at the top of your priorities list.

Remember, it's totally normal and okay to have a 'hiccup', so if you have the odd day when you're not feeling quite so chipper, that's also fine. Just make sure you take a regular step back, pause, and ask yourself, "How am I feeling and what needs to happen to make me feel my best?" Ensure you're eating regular, healthy meals, engaging in moderate exercise, and maintaining focus on a good work-life balance.

Mostly B: A Bit Blue

Okay, things have been feeling a bit "meh" recently, but well done for recognizing your current feelings. The key to coping and maintaining your well-being is to actively notice when things are starting to slip and take action.

It's important to talk to someone you trust, whether it's a friend, family member, or a counselor, about how you're feeling. Sharing your concerns may be enough to help improve your situation, but you might also consider seeking additional support, such as therapy (art, music, dance, or talk therapy), life coaching, or mindfulness classes.

Allocating enough "me" time is crucial. Think about what you would like to do to create space for yourself, just to "be" and recharge your mind and body.

Exercise is proven to help with anxiety, stress, and low mood. Eating well is also integral to maintaining a balanced mood. Don't be afraid to communicate to those around you about what you need and how they can assist you.

Mostly C: Time to Seek Help

It's truly courageous that you've been honest and open with yourself, recognizing that things are difficult. It sounds like you're struggling to cope with day-to-day life. It's essential that you don't suffer in silence or face these challenges alone. Help is always available.

Speaking to a trained counselor or therapist can be tremendously beneficial. These sessions are confidential and non-judgmental, providing you with an opportunity to unload your thoughts, address difficulties, and work towards goals to help you cope more effectively.

Without delay, confide in a trusted friend or family member about how you're feeling. There's no shame or embarrassment in seeking help; *it demonstrates bravery.* Now is not the time to be alone, and you deserve to feel better. Relaxation techniques, such as deep breathing and listening to calming, positive music, can help alleviate anxiety symptoms and improve your mood.

To put it all together, it's crucial to regularly check in with your emotional well-being. Taking this stress test can be a beneficial tool to create awareness about how you're managing your stress and emotions. Whether your results indicate you're "Feeling Good," "A Bit Blue," or it's "Time to Seek Help," remember that prioritizing your mental and emotional well-being is essential. Don't hesitate to seek support when needed, whether from trusted friends, family, or professionals. Your well-being is a priority, and you deserve to feel your best.

Proper Recovery

"Life is all about balance. You don't always need to be getting stuff done. Sometimes it's perfectly okay, and absolutely necessary, to shut down, kick back, and do nothing." — Lori Deschene

Stress and recovery are connected.

Our stress response and recovery are governed by two systems, the nervous system and the immune system. The gastrointestinal tract assumes a vital role in both the nervous system and the immune system. The well-being and operation of the GI tract can impact our stress response, and vice versa. So, let's dive into the importance of all aspects of recovery. Along the way, we'll also discuss how Lexi did with each of these categories.

Inadequate recovery from exercise can impact hormone levels in the body. Exercise, especially intense or prolonged physical activity, can trigger various hormonal responses. Proper recovery is essential for maintaining a healthy hormonal balance. Here are a few ways insufficient recovery can affect hormones:

- Cortisol Levels: Intense or prolonged exercise can elevate cortisol levels, which is a natural response to stress. However, chronic elevation of cortisol due to inadequate recovery may contribute to overtraining syndrome, which is a disruption of normal hormonal balance and leads to negative health effects.
- Testosterone Levels: Intense training followed by inadequate recovery may lead to a temporary decrease in testosterone levels.

Testosterone is essential for muscle repair and growth, so suboptimal recovery may hinder these processes.

- Insulin Sensitivity: Regular exercise improves insulin sensitivity, but overtraining without sufficient recovery may lead to insulin resistance. This can affect the body's ability to regulate blood sugar levels, potentially contributing to metabolic issues.
- Growth Hormone: Adequate sleep, which is a crucial aspect of recovery, plays a role in the release of growth hormone. Insufficient sleep due to poor recovery can impact the body's ability to produce growth hormone, which is essential for muscle repair and overall growth.
- Thyroid Hormones: Chronic overtraining without proper recovery may impact thyroid function. The thyroid hormones play a role in metabolism, and disruptions in their levels can affect energy levels and overall well-being.

It's crucial to emphasize the importance of rest, proper nutrition, sleep, and hydration in supporting the body's recovery processes. Balancing exercise with adequate recovery is key to maintaining a healthy hormonal profile and overall well-being. Individual responses to exercise and recovery can vary, so it's essential to pay attention to your body's signals and adjust your training and recovery strategies accordingly.

Days Off

When we live an extremely active life and make high demands on our bodies, we have to consider how, and when, we plan to add recovery time for our bodies to rest, repair, and reenergize. When we're young, our bodies will continue to work fairly efficiently even during the most stressful times. But, as we get older, our bodies are not able to bounce back as quickly or effectively. Deciding *not* to take a day off from being active, *not* getting adequate sleep, *not* replenishing our energy levels with proper nutrition, *not* stretching, and/or *not* addressing your mental and emotional states are all simply a recipe for disaster.

How much time your body needs for recovery will depend on many factors: age, gender, current body composition metrics, any physical or emotional demands on your body (including stress), as well as whether or not you're reaching adequate and proper nutrition levels, keeping good sleeping habits, etc.

There are many reasons proper recovery is important for the body and mind. If you don't allow your muscles, joints, connective tissues, central nervous system, utilized energy systems, cardiovascular system, and soft tissues time to rest and recover from strenuous physical activities, then eventually, your body is simply not going to function at its full potential.

Your body is an incredible machine that knows how to balance itself, even if you keep pushing yourself too hard. Eventually, your body may resist you.

For Lexi, the question was this: Was she giving her body enough time to recover each week, given the intense workouts she was performing on a regular basis?

She worked out Monday through Friday and took two days off during the weekend. This meant that she was giving herself enough time to recover after her workouts. The older you get, the more time your body will most likely need to recover. Lexi understood this well.

Now, let's discuss another form of recovery.

Sleep Quality

"Tired minds don't plan well. Sleep first, plan later." — Walter Reisch

Sleep is an essential part of our recovery process.

We must all recharge our batteries. Not the battery for your smartphone, but the one for your body.

This means *rest*. Part of recovery is encapsulated in sleep. It is important to maintain quality rituals that help you prepare for sleep and maintain adequate sleep and do so consistently. This includes calming your body and mind at a certain time in the evening and avoiding stimulating activities.

Humans have multiple biological clocks within our bodies each serving a different function.

Your circadian clock regulates various biological processes that operate on roughly a 24-hour cycle. This clock is responsible for controlling the sleep-wake cycle, body temperature, hormone production, and other physiological functions.

The sleep-wake cycle is influenced by the circadian clock, but it is also influenced by external factors such as exposure to light and darkness. Light exposure helps synchronize the circadian clock with the natural day-night cycle. Darkness promotes the release of melatonin, a hormone that prepares the body for sleep.

Your central, peripheral, and cellular clocks are subcomponents of the circadian system. Your central clock is located in the brain, primarily in the suprachiasmatic nucleus (SCN) of the hypothalamus. This is the master clock that helps regulate the timing of various physiological processes and influences the sleep-wake cycle. Your peripheral clock is found in various tissues and organs throughout the body. Peripheral clocks help coordinate local processes and ensure that different parts of the body are in sync with the central clock. They play a role in regulating things like metabolism and hormone release. Your cellular clock is an individual cell in the body containing its own internal clock. All three of these cellular clocks help manage processes within the cell and ensure that they are synchronized with the central and peripheral clocks.

All of these internal clocks coordinate and control our biological processes, such as:

- Appetite and hunger
- Body temperature
- Digestion and nutrient absorption
- Energy levels and overall alertness
- Growth, maturation, and aging
- Heart rate and rhythms
- Immunity and tissue repair
- Mood and emotions
- Releasing hormones

Modern technology can influence our internal clocks. Many of us have heard that our smartphone or tablet emits blue light wavelengths that keep the mind stimulated. Blue light, particularly in the evening or at night, can have a disruptive effect on our body's ability to relax and fall asleep. Exposure to blue light suppresses the release of melatonin, a hormone that helps regulate sleep-wake cycles.[35]

Other cues that can affect our rhythms include:

- Ambient temperature
- Eating
- Physical exertion
- Seasons
- Sensory stimuli (odors, sounds, etc.)
- Social engagements

It is important to note that sleep plays a crucial role in regulating the metabolism at a fundamental level.

Sufficient and high-quality sleep aids us in:

- Cleansing and eliminating waste products
- Gaining muscle
- Losing fat
- Recovery and repair
- Regulating blood sugar and blood lipids
- Regulating hormones
- Regulating hunger, appetite, and satiety

And, of course, the quality of our sleep significantly affects our body's ability to regulate hormones in the body.

Getting enough sleep is super important for keeping your stress levels in check. When you don't get quality sleep, it messes with your cortisol levels, which help you handle stress. So, if you're not catching enough Z's, your cortisol levels can go up, throwing off your body's natural rhythm for when it should release cortisol. And that can mean more stress and possibly some health problems down the line.

The majority of growth hormone is released when you're in deep sleep, especially in the first part of the night. But if your sleep is all over the place or not enough, it can mess with how much of this hormone you get. This can really affect your body's ability to repair tissues, build muscle, and support overall growth and development.

Getting good sleep helps your body stay sensitive to insulin. But if your sleep routine is off, it can mess with that sensitivity, leading to something called insulin resistance. This increases your chances of dealing with metabolic issues, like type 2 diabetes.

Sleep deprivation can disrupt the balance of appetite-regulating hormones—leptin and ghrelin. This imbalance can lead to increased feelings of hunger and a preference for high-calorie foods, potentially contributing to weight gain.

Sleep problems can alter your reproductive hormones, causing issues like irregular menstrual cycles in women and changes in testosterone levels in men. Addressing sleep disturbances is important since they can impact your overall hormonal balance.

Lastly, when your sleep quality isn't up to par, it can mess with the production of melatonin, which is super important for regulating your sleep-wake cycles. If your melatonin levels are off, it can make it tough to fall asleep and stay on a regular sleep schedule.

Bottom line, if there's never any focus on recovery, you will eventually burn out. It doesn't matter who you are, how strong you are, or your past experiences. Ultimately, your body may "put on the brakes."

If you aren't able to increase your sleep time, there are many other ways to relax, rejuvenate your mind, and feel reenergized. Some people do yoga, meditate, pray, read a book in a quiet place, take a hot bath, and so forth. Be proactive in finding effective rituals to help you rest and recover. This is extremely important.

For Lexi, she was getting enough quality sleep each night and waking up feeling rested and refreshed. She was getting seven hours of sleep each night, went to bed at the same time each night, and woke up at generally the same time each morning (barring unexpected situations), keeping her internal clocks in balance. She felt refreshed and energized the majority of the time.

"Lack of sleep is only bad if you have to drive, or think, or talk, or move."
— Dov Davidoff

Hydration

“Healthy, hydrated cells are the key to ageless skin and a healthy body.” — Howard Murad, MD

Every single cell and tissue in your body needs water to work properly, and guess what? Your body is about 60-70% water. It’s fascinating how crucial it is for our physical and cognitive functions to have an adequate intake of water.

Surprisingly, a significant number of individuals tend to fall short in meeting their water consumption needs. By not drinking enough water, they unknowingly deprive themselves of numerous benefits, impacting their overall well-being and performance.

Water serves these vital functions in the body:

- Blood pressure management
- Cellular function support
- Digestion support
- Joint lubrication
- Metabolism support
- Nutrient transportation
- Organ cushioning
- skin health management
- Temperature regulation
- Waste removal

Everyone's needs for water will vary based on their height, weight, age, gender, activity levels, and other physical demands. Climate and where you live will also affect your body's hydration requirements, as can other factors.

Your body's water is lost through the skin, lungs, gastrointestinal tract, and kidneys. Larger people need more water than smaller people. Sick people who are losing water through diarrhea or vomiting need more fluid and electrolytes. You need more water if it's hotter or dryer outside. If you're doing intense workouts, you'll need more water than someone who is sedentary.

We also get thirsty if we eat something salty, drink alcohol, or sweat. We are less thirsty when it's colder, humid, or when we haven't been sweating much.

It is important to note that alcohol rapidly dehydrates us. Due to its impact on an antidiuretic hormone, alcohol leads to water loss at a rate exceeding our ability to replenish it. Even if we consume water alongside alcohol, the amount lost will still surpass what we can restore for several hours. The consumption of alcohol can also inhibit the function of hormones responsible for regulating thirst and maintaining proper body water balance.

If your muscle bellies – the main part of the skeletal muscle that contracts and contains the muscle fibers responsible for generating force and movement – are not properly hydrated, they can be depleted. This ends up throwing off your entire body composition and muscle-to-fat mass ratio, and therefore impacting your body fat percentage. This is only one aspect of the importance of managing proper hydration levels and fluid balance.

It is important to be aware of the fact that dehydration can influence hormone levels in the body. Water is essential for various physiological processes, and changes in hydration status can affect hormone secretion and regulation. Here are some ways dehydration can affect hormones:

- Vasopressin (Antidiuretic Hormone – ADH): Dehydration triggers the release of vasopressin, an antidiuretic hormone that helps the body retain water by reducing urine output. Increased vasopressin levels can lead to concentrated urine and water conservation.
- Renin Angiotensin Aldosterone System (RAAS): Dehydration can activate this system, which regulates blood pressure and fluid balance. Aldosterone, a hormone produced in response to dehydration, promotes sodium retention and potassium excretion to conserve water.
- Cortisol: Chronic dehydration can lead to increased cortisol levels. This stress hormone plays a role in fluid and electrolyte balance and can be influenced by the body's hydration status.
- Thirst Sensation: This is triggered by dehydration, which prompts an individual to drink more fluids. Thirst is regulated by various hormones, including angiotensin II and aldosterone, which help stimulate the desire to increase fluid intake.
- Insulin: Some studies suggest that dehydration might mess with how sensitive your body is to insulin, which could mess with how your body handles glucose. But, we still need more studies to really nail down the connection between hydration and insulin function.

Keep in mind these potential changes and symptoms. If you are dehydrated, you might experience headaches, fatigue, difficulty focusing, low blood pressure, dizziness and/or fainting, nausea, flushing, or a rapid heart rate.[36]

When it comes to making sure you are staying hydrated each day, know that the amount of water you need will be personal to you. Most adults consume approximately 3 liters (12 cups) of fluid per day. Out of this total, about 1 liter (4 cups) is obtained from food sources, while the remaining 2 liters (8 cups) should come from beverages. I recommend discussing hydration with an experienced consultant – such as a doctor, dietitian, or nutritionist – to better understand your body's appropriate needs.

When it came to reviewing what Lexi's body needed for adequate hydration, we found she was consuming appropriate amounts of water to keep her hydrated, even with her intense workouts, which was great!

Gender-specific Hormones

"A pure heart and mind only takes you so far – sooner or later the hormones have their say, too." — Jim Butcher

Both men and women experience physical, emotional, and intellectual "mid-life" changes. This is normal; women experience menopause, and men experience andropause. These hormone changes decrease the production of sex hormones (and other hormones) as we get older.

These changes can affect:

- Body composition and lean mass (bone, connective tissue, and muscle)
- Body weight and distribution of body fat
- Digestion and gastrointestinal health
- Energy, fatigue, and sleep
- Inflammation and healing
- Mental clarity, mood, and outlook on life

Perimenopause, also known as the "around menopause" phase, is when your body goes through the natural transition leading up to menopause. It's the time when your reproductive years are starting to come to an end. If you're a woman, once you've gone a whole year without a menstrual cycle, that's when menopause officially starts and the perimenopause period ends.

Common signs of perimenopause or menopause[37] are:

- Disrupted or absent menstrual cycle
- Disrupted sleeping patterns or insomnia
- Hot flashes
- Pain during intercourse
- Mood swings, irritability
- Night sweats
- Vaginal dryness or itching

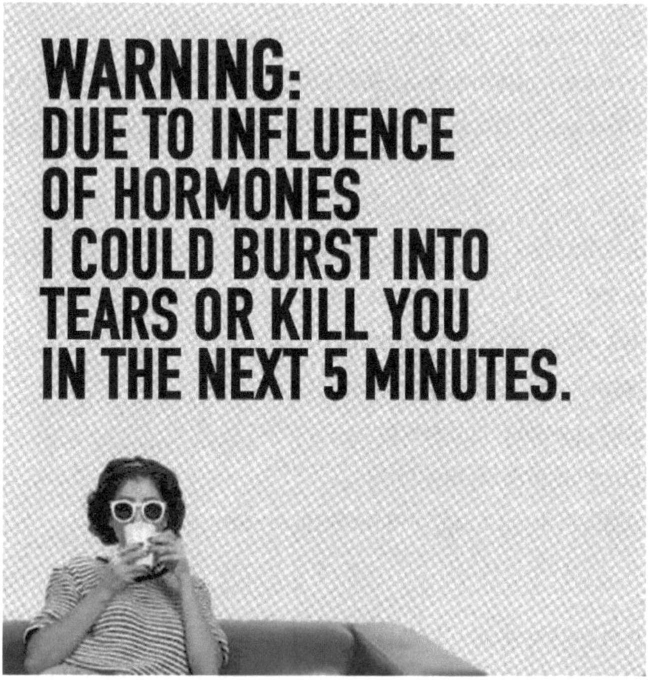

Pinterest.com[38]

Other factors that *affect* a woman's hormone homeostasis are things like getting enough sleep, managing stress, staying active, avoiding sugars, consuming healthy fats (including plenty of fatty fish), consuming appropriate amounts of dietary fiber, avoiding overeating, and, if a smoker, quitting.[37]

For men, testosterone levels typically decrease with age, which can result in them burning fewer calories each day. This decline is known as age-related hypogonadism or andropause. The average decline in testosterone levels in men is approximately 1% per year after the age of 30.[39] This decline increases to 1.3% per year in men aged 40 to 70.[40]

Of course, individual variations in testosterone levels can occur, and not all men will experience significant declines, but the decrease in these levels can contribute to weight gain.

For women, a host of physiological changes take place, whether they have children or not. Menopause is a natural biological process that typically occurs in women between the ages of 45 and 55, this marking the end of their reproductive years.

This time in a woman's life is associated with a decline in ovarian function, leading to a decrease in the production of estrogen and progesterone. These hormone fluctuations can contribute to shifts in fat distribution and metabolism, sleep disturbances, mood changes, and changes in bone health.[41]

Menopause is also associated with an increased risk of weight gain and changes in body composition. A study published in *Obstetrics and Gynecology* titled "Changes in Body Composition and Weight During the Menopause Transition" reported these findings:

- Average weight gain: Women may experience an average weight gain of 0.5 to 2 kilograms (1.1 to 4.4 pounds) during menopause.
- Abdominal fat accumulation: Menopause is associated with an increase in abdominal fat deposition. Women tend to experience a redistribution of fat from the hips and thighs to the abdominal area.

- Loss of lean body mass: A decline in lean body mass can contribute to changes in body composition and metabolism.[42]

A woman's individual experiences with weight gain during menopause can vary. Lifestyle factors such as diet, exercise, and overall health play a role in weight management.

Hormone *imbalances* occur when the body produces too much or too little of any particular hormone, but all of the different hormones work collectively in the body. So, an imbalance of one hormone can disrupt another.

To restore hormone balance, *avoid* foods that are inflammatory: refined grains, trans fats, added sugar, and certain dairy products. Frequently consuming such foods can release high amounts of insulin. When insulin is high, this prevents the release of hormones that break down stored fat for energy and can make it more difficult to burn fat throughout the day.

But, there are practical, natural solutions out there.

It's crucial to emphasize the importance of consuming adequate **protein**, especially for women between the ages of 35–55. Protein is essential for maintaining muscle mass, supporting overall health, and aiding in weight management. The recommended daily intake of protein for women in this age group varies based on factors such as activity level, overall health, and individual needs. However, a general guideline is to aim for approximately 0.8 to 1 gram of protein per kilogram of body weight.

Ensuring an adequate protein intake can contribute to:

- Preservation of lean muscle mass
- Support for metabolic function

- Support for hormone production
- Enhanced feelings of satiety, aiding in weight management

Include protein-rich foods such as lean meats, poultry, fish, eggs, dairy products, legumes, nuts, and seeds in your daily diet, which is essential for meeting protein needs. Individual variations and specific health conditions may require adjustments.

Include sources of **healthy fats** in your diet, such as avocados, nuts, seeds, and olive oil. Healthy fats are essential for hormone production and can help maintain hormonal balance.

Healthy fats are essential because they maintain:

- Cholesterol Synthesis: Cholesterol is a precursor for the synthesis of sex hormones such as testosterone, estrogen, and progesterone.
- Cellular Structure: Fats are crucial for cell membrane structure and hormone signaling. By maintaining the integrity of cell membranes, they influence the cell's responsiveness to hormonal signals, contributing to effective hormonal communication.
- Fat-Soluble Vitamins: Vitamins like A, D, E, and K, essential for hormones, are fat-soluble.
- Insulin Sensitivity: Improved insulin sensitivity is essential for regulating blood sugar levels and preventing insulin resistance, which can impact hormonal balance, especially in relation to metabolism.
- Anti-Inflammatory Effects: Omega-3s have anti-inflammatory effects, helping to reduce chronic inflammation in the body. Inflammation can disrupt hormonal balance, and by mitigating this, omega-3s support overall hormonal health.

- Brain Function: The brain is rich in omega-3 fatty acids, particularly DHA (docosahexaenoic acid). Omega-3s are vital for cognitive function and influence the regulation of hormones through the brain, specifically in areas like the hypothalamus and pituitary gland.
- Sex Hormone Production: Omega-3s play a role in the synthesis of sex hormones, including estrogen and progesterone. This is significant for maintaining reproductive health and hormonal balance.
- Gene Expression: Omega-3s may influence gene expression related to hormonal pathways. They can modulate the activity of genes involved in inflammation, metabolism, and hormonal regulation.

Incorporate omega-3 fatty acids, found in fatty fish (salmon, mackerel), flaxseeds, chia seeds, and walnuts.

Consume a variety of colorful **fruits and vegetables** rich in antioxidants. Antioxidants help maintain hormonal balance through their ability to counteract oxidative stress in the body.

Antioxidants contribute to hormonal health by:

- Combat Oxidative Stress: Antioxidants neutralize free radicals, which are unstable molecules that can cause oxidative stress. Oxidative stress has been linked to disruptions in hormonal balance.
- Protection of Hormone-Producing Glands: Hormone-producing glands, such as the thyroid and adrenal glands, are vulnerable to oxidative damage. Antioxidants help protect these glands, ensuring proper hormone production and release.

- Preservation of Cell Receptors: Hormones exert their effects by binding to specific receptors on cell surfaces. Oxidative stress can damage these receptors, impairing the cell's ability to respond to hormonal signals. Antioxidants help preserve the integrity of these receptors.
- Reduction of Inflammation: Chronic inflammation can interfere with hormonal balance. Antioxidants, by mitigating inflammation, indirectly contribute to maintaining proper hormone levels.
- Support for Reproductive Health: Antioxidants play a role in supporting reproductive health by protecting eggs and sperm from oxidative damage. This is crucial for maintaining fertility and hormonal balance.
- Inactivation of Endocrine Disruptors: Antioxidants may help neutralize endocrine-disrupting chemicals that can interfere with hormonal regulation. By neutralizing these disruptors, antioxidants contribute to overall hormonal stability.
- Aging and Hormonal Changes: Antioxidants may slow down the aging process and reduce age-related hormonal changes. They help protect cells from damage over time, supporting the maintenance of hormonal balance.

Fiber helps regulate insulin levels and may influence hormone balance. High-fiber foods contribute to maintaining hormonal balance through several mechanisms:

- Insulin Regulation: Fiber slows down the digestion and absorption of carbohydrates, helping to regulate blood sugar levels. This, in turn, supports insulin sensitivity and helps prevent insulin spikes, promoting overall hormonal balance.

- Gut Health: Fiber is essential for a healthy gut microbiota. A balanced and diverse gut microbiome influences the production of hormones, such as those related to appetite and metabolism. This microbial balance is crucial for hormonal regulation.
- Estrogen Metabolism: Certain types of dietary fiber, such as lignans found in flaxseeds, may assist in the metabolism of estrogen. This can be particularly relevant for hormonal balance in women.
- Appetite Regulation: High-fiber foods contribute to a feeling of fullness and satiety. This helps regulate appetite and prevents overeating, which can have positive effects on hormones involved in metabolism and weight regulation.
- Balancing Sex Hormones: Fiber can play a role in balancing sex hormones, such as estrogen and testosterone, by aiding in their excretion from the body. This is important for maintaining reproductive health and hormonal equilibrium.
- Inflammation Reduction: Chronic inflammation can disrupt hormonal balance. High-fiber diets have been associated with lower levels of inflammation, indirectly supporting hormonal health.
- Stabilizing Cortisol Levels: Fiber can contribute to stabilizing cortisol levels, the hormone associated with stress. By modulating stress hormones, fiber helps maintain a more balanced hormonal profile.

Include high-fiber foods like whole grains, fruits, vegetables, and legumes to support digestive health.

Phytoestrogens may have a balancing effect on estrogen levels. Phytoestrogens are plant-derived compounds that have a structure similar to estrogen, which is the primary female sex hormone.

Phytoestrogens can influence hormonal balance by:

- Estrogen-Like Effects: Phytoestrogens can bind to estrogen receptors in the body and mimic the effects of natural estrogen. This can be beneficial, especially during periods of hormonal fluctuations, helping to maintain a balance in estrogen activity.
- Adaptogenic Properties: Phytoestrogens have adaptogenic properties, meaning they can modulate hormonal activity based on the body's needs. They can act as either weak estrogens or anti-estrogens, depending on the hormonal context, contributing to overall hormonal balance.
- Competitive Inhibition: Phytoestrogens may compete with endogenous estrogen for binding to receptors. In situations of excess estrogen or hormonal imbalances, they can help regulate estrogen activity by competitively inhibiting stronger estrogenic effects.
- Selective Estrogen Receptor Modulation (SERM): Phytoestrogens exhibit SERM properties, acting selectively on estrogen receptors. This selective action allows them to modulate estrogenic effects in different tissues, contributing to a more balanced hormonal environment.
- Potential Anti-Cancer Effects: Some studies suggest that phytoestrogens may have protective effects against hormone-related cancers, possibly by influencing hormonal balance. This includes potential benefits in breast and prostate cancer prevention.

- Bone Health: Phytoestrogens may contribute to maintaining bone health by exerting estrogen-like effects on bone metabolism. This is particularly relevant during periods of hormonal changes, such as menopause.

Include foods rich in phytoestrogens, such as soy products, flaxseeds, and whole grains.

Ingesting an adequate intake of **vitamins and minerals** is crucial for maintaining hormonal balance as these micronutrients play various roles in hormone synthesis, regulation, and overall cellular function. Some of this information has already been mentioned, but this section highlights the benefits specific to vitamins and minerals.

Vitamins and minerals contribute to hormonal balance by:

- Cofactors in Hormone Synthesis: Many vitamins and minerals serve as cofactors in the synthesis of hormones. Again, vitamin D is essential for the production of steroid hormones like testosterone and estrogen, while iodine is necessary for the synthesis of thyroid hormones.
- Antioxidant Protection: Remember certain vitamins, such as vitamin C and E, and minerals like selenium, act as antioxidants. They help protect hormone-producing glands, such as the thyroid and adrenal glands, from oxidative damage, ensuring proper hormone production.
- Regulation of Blood Sugar: Minerals like chromium and magnesium play a role in insulin sensitivity and glucose metabolism. Maintaining optimal blood sugar levels is crucial for hormonal balance, especially in relation to insulin and cortisol.
- Thyroid Function: Iodine, selenium, and zinc are essential for thyroid function. The thyroid gland produces hormones that

regulate metabolism, energy balance, and overall hormonal stability.

- Conversion of Precursors: Some vitamins, such as B-vitamins (e.g., B6, B12, folate), are involved in the conversion of hormone precursors into their active forms. This is important for the synthesis and regulation of various hormones.
- Bone Health and Hormones: Vitamins D and K, along with minerals like calcium and phosphorus, contribute to bone health. Adequate bone health is linked to hormonal balance, particularly in postmenopausal women.
- Immune System Support: Vitamins and minerals support the immune system, and a healthy immune system is crucial for overall well-being, including hormonal health.
- Anti-Inflammatory Effects: Some vitamins and minerals, like vitamin E and zinc, have anti-inflammatory properties. Chronic inflammation can disrupt hormonal balance, and these nutrients contribute to a reduction in inflammatory processes.

Ensure adequate intake of vitamins and minerals, particularly vitamin D, vitamin B6, vitamin E, magnesium, and zinc.

Instead of adding a probiotic to your daily routine, add in **probiotic-rich foods**, which contain beneficial bacteria, can influence hormonal balance, and other mechanisms.

Probiotics may contribute to maintaining hormonal balance by:

- Gut Microbiota Influence: Probiotics contribute to a healthy balance of gut microbiota. The gut microbiome plays a crucial role in modulating the endocrine system and influencing the production and regulation of hormones.

- Serotonin Production: A significant portion of serotonin, a neurotransmitter with hormone-like effects, is produced in the gut. Probiotics can influence serotonin production, which can have positive effects on mood, appetite, and sleep regulation.
- Cortisol Regulation: The gut-brain axis, the bidirectional communication between the gut and the brain, is influenced by probiotics. This communication can impact the regulation of stress hormones, such as cortisol, contributing to a more balanced stress response.
- Inflammation Reduction: Probiotics have anti-inflammatory properties and can help maintain a balanced inflammatory response in the gut. Chronic inflammation can disrupt hormonal balance, and a healthy gut environment may mitigate this disruption.
- Estrogen Metabolism: Some probiotics may play a role in modulating estrogen metabolism in the gut. This can be relevant for hormonal balance, especially in relation to sex hormones.
- Insulin Sensitivity: There is emerging evidence suggesting that the gut microbiota, influenced by probiotics, may play a role in improving insulin sensitivity. This can contribute to hormonal balance, particularly in relation to blood sugar regulation
- Short-Chain Fatty Acid Production: Probiotics contribute to the production of short-chain fatty acids (SCFAs) in the gut. SCFAs have been implicated in various physiological processes, including hormone regulation and metabolic health.

Incorporate probiotic-rich foods like yogurt, kefir, pickles (fermented in brine), miso, sauerkraut, tempeh, and kimchi.

These have been shown to potentially help regulate hormones:

- Black Cohosh: This herb can help reduce hot flashes, excessive sweating, sleep disturbances, mood swings, irritability, bone density loss, reduced mental performance, and risk of heart disease.
- Red Clover: This herb may improve bone health and may help with anxiety and depression.
- Borage Oil: This oil contains fatty acid GLA, which is an anti-inflammatory & may reduce joint pain. It may have an antioxidant effect, as well.
- St. John's Wort: This is an herbal supplement that research suggests may aid in reducing symptoms associated with menopause, including hot flashes and depression.
- Licorice Root: This item may help with skin inflammation, GI irritation, and ulcers.
- Valerian Root: This plant has mild sedative properties and is reported to be a sleep aid (helping one fall asleep faster and/or get better-quality sleep), as well as relieve restlessness and other anxiety symptoms.

It is important to note that everyone's body is unique and individual results will vary.

When it came to Lexi's hormone levels, we discovered – through discussing her symptoms and reviewing her food choices – that her hormones were the cause of her plateau. She was at the perimenopause stage in her life.

Lexi's body was experiencing the signs, but she didn't know how to correct this. Together, one of the things we focused on was making sure she was consuming enough healthy protein sources and dietary fats.

Once we fine-tuned her food choices, I encouraged her to start on an all-natural hormone stabilizer. After about a month, she began to feel amazing results. Her hot flashes and horrible cramps stopped. She wasn't only feeling better but feeling the best she'd felt in a long time, with her energy levels soaring. And, just as important for her, she was seeing weight loss progress once again.

When it comes to all of the factors that are the key to your success, all of them being *critical* to success, you can ensure compliance with two, three, or even four factors and still not quite reach your full potential. Lexi was doing great with four out of five. Through a little discovery, setting goals together, and putting those goals into practice, we had her excelling at five out of five!

When you focus on aligning all five of these key components in your life, you give yourself the best opportunity to achieve your full potential in terms of your health goals.

Mental + Emotional Health

"Life isn't about waiting for the storm to pass; it's about learning how to dance in the rain." — Vivian Greene

Having mental and emotional health means more than the absence of mental illness or the ability to control one's emotions. It's a state of well-being that allows you to cope with stresses in life, realize your abilities, and learn, work, and contribute to society. It signifies our individual and collective abilities to make decisions, make and build relationships, and shape the path our lives take.

Mental and emotional health are both crucial human rights. Unfortunately, mental and emotional health are both in an overall decline. Around the globe, an estimated 280 million individuals experience depression. The prevalence of depression among women is approximately 50% higher compared to men.[43]

Negative emotions are a natural part of human experience, and most people will experience them at some point. Some negative emotions are:

- Anger
- Anxiety
- Disgust
- Fear
- Frustration
- Guilt
- Hopelessness
- Insecurity

- Jealousy
- Loneliness
- Regret
- Sadness

Experiencing these is not necessarily considered a bad thing. Negative emotions can serve as signals, helping individuals recognize problems, make necessary changes, or seek support and solutions to improve their overall well-being.

In our hectic lifestyles, maintaining our mental and emotional health is essential for our overall health and quality of life. When it comes to these components, self-care plays a huge role in preventing an unhealthy mindset. The NIH (National Institutes of Health) offers healthy options for maintaining mental and emotional health:

- Exercise regularly
- Consume regular, healthy meals
- Stay hydrated
- Make sleep a priority
- Partake in relaxing activities
- Set goals and understand your priorities
- Practice gratitude
- Focus on a positivity
- Stay connected[44]

Psychological research on emotions identifies a core list of positive emotions which are commonly experienced by most people across different cultures and contexts. They are:

- Admiration
- Amusement
- Awe
- Compassion
- Excitement
- Gratitude
- Happiness
- Hope
- Joy
- Love
- Pride
- Serenity[45]

Positive emotions play a big role in keeping your mind and heart in good shape. Having a mix of positive emotions is key to living a healthy and fulfilling life.

By understanding how positive emotions impact our well-being, we can better appreciate the intricate relationship between our emotional states and other factors influencing our potential.

As previously mentioned, we know that, for women, our emotions can be affected by our hormones. Hopefully, now you are seeing the connectedness of all of the *secrets to your full potential*. One component can absolutely affect the other.

So, before attempting to take on new goals, we must be cognitive of whether our mental and emotional states are in a healthy place. If they are not, we need to take action steps in order to bring our mind and emotions back to homeostasis.

The NIH also provides different wellness checklists that can help people proactively manage the different aspects of health. Here is what they list:

Physical Wellness Checklist:

- Get active
- Build and maintain muscle
- Choose healthy food choices
- Understand your metabolism
- Create healthy habits
- Discover what your healthy weight is[46]

Emotional Wellness Checklist:

- Be resilient
- Manage stress
- Get quality sleep
- Be mindful
- Cope with loss
- Deepen social connections[47]

Social Wellness Checklist:

- Build connections
- Self-care while caring for others
- Get active with others
- Create healthy habits for your family
- Maintain a bond with your kids

- Nurture healthy relationships[48]

Environmental Wellness Checklist:

- Make your home healthier
- Reduce allergens
- Create smart habits in a hot climate
- Protect yourself against cold weather
- Maintain healthy air quality
- Remove in-home toxins
- Exercise water safety[49]

These suggestions are listed in order to create awareness and promote being proactive in at least some of these arenas of health. Again, these are all things we typically don't think about, which is why I bring them to your attention. Addressing some or all of these elements can help set you up with a great foundation before you begin attacking your new goals and priorities.

Takeaways from Lexi

The key takeaways from Lexi's story are the five critical components of success involved in achieving optimal health. These are the keys to reaching your full potential that most people tend to overlook or ignore.

Now that you are aware of these critical factors, you can at the very least keep them in mind when setting goals based on your priorities. Once you start implementing the action steps towards reaching your goals, but find that progress has stalled, review these key points to see if the "missing link" to your success lies within one of these areas. Because, if you are experiencing hormone imbalances – and this includes stress hormones –it will negatively affect your ability to lose weight. Until steps are taken to balance hormones or manage stress, you may very well stay in a plateau.

However, don't despair, right now we're going to uncover what you are currently doing to unlock your full potential and what areas need attention so you can improve. It's important to take a closer look at your habits and actions to understand what's working and what needs a bit of attention. This process is all about helping you make positive changes to improve your overall health and well-being.

Now, let's zoom in on your current actions – the things you're doing right now that contribute to unlocking your full potential. This exploration will not only celebrate your strengths and successes but also identify specific areas that could use a little extra attention.

Think of it as a friendly guide, helping you navigate your unique journey towards better health. Embrace this opportunity to understand and address different aspects of your well-being. It's not just about overcoming challenges; it's about creating a roadmap that empowers you to enhance your overall health, leading to a happier and more fulfilling life. Every positive step you take is a win, and with each improvement, you're moving closer to realizing your full potential.

So, let's embark on this journey together, making positive changes one step at a time!

Self-Discovery: Are You Living Your Potential?

When most of us think about getting healthy, we usually focus our efforts on improving our nutrition and increasing our physical activity. While this is a great way to start, we cannot forget to review every aspect of our health. Let's take a moment to check in with our bodies and see if there is any room for improvement.

Stress Management:

1. What are you *currently doing* to relieve stress?
2. What have you tried doing *in the past* to relieve stress?
3. What do you think you could do now to *manage* stress levels?

Exercise Recovery:

1. What are you *currently doing* for exercise recovery?
2. What have you tried *in the past* for exercise recovery?
3. What do you think you could do now to *manage* exercise recovery?

Sleep Quality:

4. What are you *currently doing* to ensure good sleep quality?
5. What have you tried *in the past* to ensure good sleep quality?
6. What do you think you could do now to *manage* sleep quality?

Hydration:

4. What are you *currently doing* to stay hydrated?
5. What have you tried *in the past* to stay hydrated?
6. What do you think you could do now to *manage* hydration?

Hormone Levels:

7. What are you *currently doing* to maintain hormone balance?
8. What have you tried *in the past* to maintain hormone balance?
9. What do you think you could do now to *manage* your hormones?

Mental + Emotional Health:

7. What are you *currently doing* to ensure good M + E Health?
8. What have you tried *in the past* to ensure good M + E Health??
9. What do you think you could do to *manage* your M + E Health?

If you have already incorporated daily habits to address these areas on a regular basis, awesome job! Seriously, bravo!

Meanwhile, brainstorming the answers to these questions will allow you to create opportunities when you feel like one or more of these issues are affecting your ability to achieve progress.

If you find yourself in a weight loss plateau, your hormones (women-specific, thyroid, and stress-related) are areas that need to be addressed. Most individuals underestimate how influential your hormones are on your body. If there are any imbalances, your body will eventually "put on the brakes."

Do not neglect these areas of your life. If you do, you will be unable to reach your full potential. And my goal is to give you every opportunity to reach your full potential!

Part 6

Set Yourself up for Success

"Who you are tomorrow begins with what you do today." — Tim Fargo

Perhaps the one question I am most often asked is, "*How do I set myself up for success?*"

I talk about success throughout this book. Naturally, when you're aiming to change your life to achieve optimal health and a healthy lifestyle, you want to be successful.

Everyone is going to measure success differently, but it's like building a house. If you don't have a strong foundation, you might be able to build the house, move in, and enjoy living there for a while, but eventually the structure will collapse.

This is the same concept to have in mind when trying to positively change your life.

I want you to live the amazing life that you deserve. You are an amazing person, and I want to help you achieve your health goals and live with energy and vitality for many more years! In order for you to do that, you need to understand the best way to set yourself up for success.

We explored the "above the belt" key points in the first part of this book. In this context, *above the belt* essentially refers to your foundation and everything that embodies you: your purpose, vision, mission, goals, and standards, and so forth. Above the belt is where your heart is.

The remainder of this book will focus on the last five "below the belt" key points for achieving success. In this context, *below the belt* pertains to the tools or tactics that can assist you in taking action and implementing what you have learned about accomplishing your goals. Below the belt are your legs that serve as the driving force that propels you into action.

Now, as we go through these remaining sections, really try to understand how to implement them into your life. Use what you've already learned from this book to help you succeed with these steps. It's all starting to come together, and these remaining sections will allow you to put everything into action.

Know Your Priorities

"You always have time for the things you put first." — *Unknown*

Understanding your biggest, most important priorities and setting appropriate, realistic behavior-based goals are two key components in setting yourself up for success.

There is a distinction when we mention setting appropriate and realistic goals based on your priorities. You can have appropriate goals, but are they also realistic? They might very well be appropriate for you, your skills, your age, your health, and so on, but depending on your career, family responsibilities and obligations, location, budget, and so on, they might not be realistic, at least not at this time.

Therefore, our ultimate objective is to create goals that are both appropriate and realistic.

As mentioned in Part 3, based on your priorities, make sure you have one big, overarching outcome-based goal in mind.

Having at least one larger, overarching goal is just as important as having your smaller milestone goals. But, keep in mind, your focus always stays on your smaller milestone goals; never your overarching outcome-based goal.

To explain this more, let's discuss Nina.

Meet Nina

Like most moms, Nina was incredibly busy when we met. She was the typical supermom – working, running her kids to school, to soccer practice, to dance recitals, and to their friends' houses, as well as making breakfast and dinner every day.

She never complained about it, as most mothers don't. She loved her children and would do anything for them. She absolutely loved being a mother. What brought her to me was that she wanted to lose weight but couldn't figure out how in the world she was going to do that, fitting self-care into her demanding schedule.

She was a kind and compassionate woman in her early 30s. She had two children, and she wanted to show them it was possible to do all this and still take care of herself.

Remember, when you are trying to solidify new, healthy habits, that it is not about *what* you do, but *how* you do it.

While I talked with Nina, I recognized that she was expecting perfection: The perfect workout routine for a minimum of five days a week, perfect food choices for her and her family, perfectly fitting this into her "insane" schedule, and of course, for her progress to jumpstart right away.

For the majority of us who are extremely busy, setting that kind of standard or expectation for ourselves can quickly become discouraging. When our plate is already full and it seems like we have no time whatsoever for anything else, this can easily become overwhelming for any one of us.

That's not to say your goals are impossible, though!

Let me just tell you, *"You've got this!"*

You can do it.

I believe in you.

But remember, you must keep things simple.

I sat with Nina and together we went over what was truly important to her. Yes, losing weight was important. Staying active, getting healthy, and having more energy were important. But everyone has something that is *the most important goal* for them.

What I have discovered throughout the years is that when I ask clients what their most important goal is, or why they reached out to me, the first answer a person comes up with is usually not what's truly important. It's often a superficial answer. You have to dig deep and explore your true self. You have to brainstorm, write down the ideas that come to mind, let them simmer, and then focus on the ones that pop out the most (for you, not what you believe someone else thinks is important for you).

Once Nina had her list of priorities in hand, we were able to select a couple of the most important ones to initially focus on.

First, she wanted to actually make your priorities a priority. With most adults being extremely busy, our schedules need to have some flexibility, but too much can cause our days to feel chaotic and out of control. When there's no routine, we're not being as efficient with our time as we could be and are therefore accomplishing less. Nina was aware of this and knew that simply making her priorities a priority would significantly improve her and her family's life.

Secondly, being incredibly busy, she wasn't able to actually make time for self-care. She would tell herself each day to set aside time for self-care, but she'd never get around to it. It was always pushed to the next day. At the end of each day, she would think to herself, "I'll get to it tomorrow." She recognized this repeated action and knew it was important for her to work on it. She knew adding self-care to her schedule would not only benefit her, but her entire family, as well. It would help balance out the busy moments that required more of her energy, help manage her stress levels, improve her mood, and allow her to focus more on positivity, appreciation, and her blessings.

These were the two things that were most important for her to focus on in the beginning.

Everyone needs to start somewhere. It is extremely important to try not to conquer everything at once.

When you are incredibly busy and feel like you have no spare time whatsoever, try reviewing your calendar and deciding when or how you can fit things in. In reality, it only takes a few minutes to figure this out.

I asked Nina, "When is the best time for you to *plan and prepare*, that allows you to accomplish your top priorities?"

The answer to this question is going to be different for everyone. It depends on the individual, the habits we are addressing, our schedule, and a host of other factors. It might be Sunday afternoon before the workweek begins.

"When is the best time for you to *work on* your top priorities?" It might be early in the morning (especially if you are an early riser) before everyone else in the household wakes up. Or, it might be late at night after everyone has gone to bed.

Then I asked, "How can you be the most *efficient with the time* designated for working on your top priorities?"

The answer to this question will also depend on the individual, the habit you are addressing, your time frame, distractions, and other factors. Each habit will require different preparation.

Planning ahead is only part of the solution. Getting and staying organized on a daily basis is vital. If you are disorganized, things are going to fall apart pretty quickly. Instead, set aside time on a regular basis to focus on the habits you are working on.

If you want to successfully solidify new habits, you cannot be indecisive and attempt to work on all of your goals at once. This is one fundamental reason why trying to create too many new, healthy habits at once generally ends up being unsuccessful. Going that route will only overwhelm you. Instead, choose a couple of goals that are deeply meaningful to you and focus your efforts on those goals first.

It is virtually impossible to make all things important to you a priority when you are trying to work out five times a week, eat healthier, practice self-love, drink more water, manage your stress, get adequate sleep, and still continue to do all of the other daily things your life demands.

Does this sound familiar?

Nina needed to stay focused by taking a few minutes every day to familiarize herself with what top priorities she was going to work on the *next* day.

Almost all of the top motivational speakers and leaders who talk about being successful say the same thing: You have to know what your day looks like when you first start out. You need to make a list of every activity, every task, every 10- or 15-minute block of time throughout your day and hold yourself to the plan.

Nina printed out her list of priorities for the day, including what her meals were going to be. This daily print-out was a constant reminder of what she still had left to achieve for that day. And, when she treated it like an assignment, at least in the beginning, it was easier for her to hold fast to those expectations and activities.

There are so many different ways to stay organized. Find the tools or tactics that work best for you. For some people, it might be reminders on their smartphone. I am a to-do list fanatic. Typically, my Post-its have Post-its, and then I have notes and reminders in my smartphone about my Post-it notes. Visually seeing that I'm crossing things off my list gives me a sense of accomplishment.

Maybe you use a traditional organizer, a calendar on your refrigerator, or an app on your smartphone. Whatever works best for you, use that. The more you understand what works best for you, the more likely you are to set yourself up for success.

Takeaways from Nina

Perhaps the most important aspect I want you to take away from Nina's story is the need for understanding not only what your health priorities are, but also your scheduling.

How do you stay on track throughout your day?

What ways help you make your top priorities a priority?

Whether you have a full-time job, a couple of part-time jobs, are a stay-at-home mom, a student, or anything else, creating a schedule or list of things to do will help you create time to develop new habits.

If you are focusing on improving your nutrition, understand your culinary *style*. Now, what do I mean by that?

To illustrate, if you are the type of person who loves to cook, you might prefer to make everything at home. But if you really don't like spending time in the kitchen, you might look for other options. While I don't recommend packaged meals, there are a lot of things that can help save time, such as a meal prep service. Just make sure you're aware of what's *in* your prepared meal.

So, are you a weekly food prepper, a daily chef, or a no-prep person? Understanding your culinary style will help you alter your nutritional habits and bring them in alignment with your daily priorities and long-term goals.

Once you have identified your overarching outcome-based goals, create smaller behavior-based action steps *in reverse order*. By regressing from achieving your goal back to your starting point with behavior-based milestones, you not only establish the necessary steps but it also ensures that you allocate sufficient time to achieve each smaller milestone.

For example, if your goal is to lose fifty pounds in a year's time, reverse-engineer the steps you need to take to get there. What are all the things you will you need to accomplish within your time frame? Know when your goal needs to be accomplished. What do your goals need to be for that last month? The month before that? Before that? And so on, until you reach your staring point.

The more you break down the steps (reverse-engineering them), the easier it will be for you to see progress and understand your path from your current position to the point of achieving your overarching goal. Make adjustments as needed.

And yes, you will need to make adjustments as you go. In most cases, it's necessary to adjust the steps we take because of a missed day, slower-than-expected progress, or some other hurdle or obstacle that's been thrown in our path.

Make sure to break everything down into stages and time frames, and you *will* get there.

Ways We Procrastinate

Are you a procrastinator? We've all procrastinated at some point in our lives. It's common. But, for some people, procrastination has become a lifestyle. And with our busy lives, we all know how challenging it can be to avoid procrastination.

If you know you have a tendency to procrastinate, especially when things get tough, acknowledge the habit and build a plan to overcome the tendency. Your accountability partner will also be able to help you with this.

On the other hand, you might very well be a preparation master. You might be someone who prepares well – and maybe even overprepares. If you have a tendency to overprepare, though, that could be just as powerful a stumbling block as procrastinating. You could spend the majority of your time and effort preparing rather than acting.

One of the reasons we may procrastinate is that the task at hand *seems to include a challenging start.* Sometimes, our minds have a way of making a task seem far more daunting than it actually is. Possibly, it's a task we don't want to start, so our minds rationalize why beginning it is simply too much to handle. But here's the thing: We can outsmart our own minds and make things more doable simply by focusing *only* on the first step.

Instead of committing to completing an arduous task all at once, start by working on it for only ten minutes. Your task will end up feeling much more doable.

By breaking things down into manageable chunks, we can overcome that initial resistance and get started on tasks that seemed overwhelming in the beginning. It's all about finding a way to lower that commitment barrier and make progress one small step at a time.

Another reason we may procrastinate is that we lie to ourselves and *believe our own rationalizations for putting things off.* We've all heard those familiar lines like, "I'll get to it tomorrow."

We have all sorts of reasons and justifications. We might convince ourselves that we thrive under the pressure of a looming deadline. Or we believe we need to wait for the right mood, or inspiration, to strike before tackling the task.

But here's the thing: "Later" never seems to arrive.

If you catch yourself uttering excuses for procrastination, then you're exhibiting the classic signs of a procrastinator. It's a behavior pattern that many of us fall into from time to time.

The way to overcome these blocks is by first being honest with yourself about why you're procrastinating. Then, acknowledge that time passes no matter what. Putting something off until later only creates more stress and anxiety. What happens if you wait until the last minute to do something, and then you're at your deadline, but there's no time? Or an emergency happens and then you really *can't* complete what you needed to? If you decide to start, even if it's a brief start, you will accomplish something which will help you feel productive, create a sense of self-pride, and promote a healthy, positive mindset.

The next reason we may procrastinate is due to *being distracted.* Proximity to distractions is a huge factor that affects our ability to stay focused on a daily basis.

Back when I was a kid, things were simpler. The computer was located in the study room. My family owned a television, but it only had local channels and we weren't allowed to watch much TV. There were no smartphones or iPads. We lived on five acres in the countryside, so life was slower.

Today, our technology is always either right in hand or within arm's reach. Distractions are constantly in our faces, and their power over us has become far stronger than we anticipated. Many of these types of distractions aren't necessary for survival, but we have allowed them to become so. It's no wonder staying on track has become such a struggle.

There are ways to fight this, though. We can turn off notifications to apps, text messages, email alerts, and so on.

We are the ones deciding to be more available to the world. Instead, create boundaries for any unimportant distractions you may have.

This is a practice I incorporated into my life several years ago. I found that I was becoming a slave to my smartphone. Every time I received an alert or notification, I would jump to see what it was for. I found myself constantly feeling anxious and stressed. I decided this wasn't healthy for me and turned off all notifications except for phone calls and text messages. Typically, my smartphone is set to 'Do Not Disturb' anyway. This allows me to be in control of reviewing notifications when the time is best for me and my schedule.

Lastly, we may procrastinate because *we haven't created a strong* ***why***. Are you struggling to find motivation? Do you find yourself caught in a cycle of avoiding action? It's possible that you're not feeling motivated because you haven't been able to gather a convincing enough argument for *why* you should kick-start your efforts. We have discussed the topic of finding your "why" – your deeper meaning – extensively in this book. This effort will also allow you to overcome obstacles when it comes to lacking motivation.

Self-Discovery: Do You Procrastinate on Priorities?

Take this quiz to find out if you fit the typical procrastinator mold. This quiz encompasses elements found in many common procrastinator quizzes.

For each statement, use the corresponding answer that best describes you. Each answer has a number value associated with it in parenthesis. Add up your score at the end and use the key to find out if you might be a procrastinator.

a. Not at All (5)
b. Rarely (4)
c. Sometimes (3)
d. Often (2)
e. All the Time (1)

1. I delay completing tasks until the last moment.
2. I only take action when an urgent situation emerges.
3. I find myself doing tasks that I had originally planned to complete the day before.
4. I avoid establishing a daily schedule to manage my time.
5. It is difficult for me to say no to requests or invitations.
6. Initiating a project or task can pose a challenge for me.
7. I have difficulty making timely decisions.
8. I often waste time engaging in unrelated activities when faced with a deadline.
9. When I become bored with a task, I divert my attention elsewhere.
10. I regularly postpone tasks and think, "I'll do it tomorrow."
11. When faced with a demanding task, I often invent excuses to delay working on that task.
12. It is rare that I accomplish what I set out to do in a given day.
13. I lack clear goals or objectives for my activities.
14. I spend a significant amount of time on social media.
15. Non-essential activities frequently divert my focus from completing my work.

Now, add up your points using the answer key provided at the beginning of this quiz. Refer to the score key below to find out how you rank in terms of procrastination.

50-75 Points

You don't exhibit consistent patterns of procrastination, which is excellent news! WOO HOO! This will only benefit your life by allowing you to stay organized and on top of things as they occur in your life. Keep up the positive habits that are keeping you proactive and preventing you from procrastinating.

30-49 Points

You tend to display mild procrastination tendencies. It's probable that you encounter moderate difficulties with avoidance and procrastination. Managing your daily tasks, meeting deadlines, and prioritizing important matters may pose challenges for you. You do have a tendency to delay and postpone crucial tasks that require completion. Additionally, you may find it challenging to resist immediate gratification.

15-29 Points

You have a tendency to procrastinate, and this behavior likely affects various aspects of your life. This could lead to missed deadlines or significant time wasted. You often leave tasks until the last minute, causing feelings of stress and being overwhelmed. Consequently, people in your life may also experience frustration as a result of your procrastinating behavior.

Try some of the suggestions this chapter offers. At the very least, try to discover why you procrastinate to better understand if there are ways to avoid this behavior through scheduling, assistance, redirection, self-love, etc. This is personal to you and situation-specific.

Below are some tips that can allow you to be proactive and will serve as a helpful refresher based on what we've already discussed:

- *Create a Structured Schedule:* Establish a daily routine with set time blocks for tasks to enhance organization and productivity.
- *Prioritize Tasks:* Identify and prioritize important tasks to ensure they are addressed promptly, reducing the likelihood of procrastination.
- *Break Tasks into Smaller Steps:* Divide larger tasks into smaller, more manageable steps, making them less overwhelming and more achievable for you.
- *Set Realistic Goals:* Establish achievable goals with clear, realistic timelines to prevent being overwhelmed.
- *Set Clear Deadlines:* Break down tasks into smaller, manageable goals with specific deadlines to avoid last-minute rushes.
- *Use Time Management Tools:* Employ tools like calendars, planners, or productivity apps to help track and manage tasks effectively.
- *Seek Accountability Partners:* Share your goals and deadlines with someone who can hold you accountable. This will provide you with an external motivator.
- *Minimize Distractions:* Create a focused work environment by minimizing distractions. This will allow for increased concentration on the tasks at hand.

- *Practice Mindfulness:* Develop mindfulness techniques to stay present and reduce the appeal of immediate gratification, which fosters better long-term decision-making.
- *Stress Reduction Techniques:* Learn and practice stress management techniques such as deep breathing, progressive muscle relaxation, or yoga to help address the emotional components contributing to your procrastination.
- *Reflect on Consequences:* Consider the potential consequences of delaying tasks, which emphasizes the importance of timely action to help avoid future challenges.
- *Visualization:* Visualize the positive outcomes of completing tasks on time to boost your motivation.
- *Routine Assessment:* Regularly reassess and adjust your routines to ensure they remain effective.
- *Learn from Setbacks:* Instead of dwelling on past procrastination, focus on learning from setbacks and adapting your approach moving forward.
- *Reward Yourself:* Incorporate a system of rewards for completing tasks on time to reinforce positive behavior and motivation.
- *Professional Help:* Consider seeking assistance from a therapist or counselor to explore the underlying causes of procrastination and develop coping strategies.

Plan & Stay Organized

"Always plan ahead. It wasn't raining when Noah built the ark."
— Anthony Robbins

Planning and staying organized are two essential keys to long-lasting success.

This is probably not new information. Most of us know this. Yet, as I mentioned earlier:

Information does not cause transformation.

Some of us still try to skip this part. Why? Because we think it takes too much time. If we *really* think about it, we'll come to the conclusion that it doesn't take that much time or effort to plan ahead and stay organized. But we tend to avoid these key elements, even though *we know* that addressing these issues provides us a greater chance of being more efficient and reaching success faster.

Why? Well, let's be real here. If you ever find yourself rationalizing or creating excuses for why you cannot properly plan for success, that should be a wakeup call. That should be the moment when you realize your goal isn't deeply meaningful to you; it's not a priority.

But that's okay, because you have discovered it is *not* an important goal to be striving for *right now*. Maybe it will be later! So, now it's about discovering what *is* truly meaningful to you at this point in time.

Anytime I have a consultation with a potential private client, I can always distinguish if they're truly ready for a healthy change. There are multiple things that help me decipher this.

The recommendation I have for these prospective clients is this: Never force it. For example, if eating healthy and getting active are not truly meaningful to you right now, don't force it. Some people may feel they have to eat healthy or are being pressured into losing weight by a family member; then, they wonder why they can't stay committed or make any successful progress. They're not doing it for the reasons that are deeply meaningful for them.

Don't force it.

I am not condoning being unhealthy or promoting a sedentary life, but we're all adults, and no one can force you to do anything you don't truly want to do.

Instead of trying to force yourself to eat healthy, maybe the key for you is not to change *what* you are eating, but *how much* you are eating. Oftentimes, simply focusing on portion sizes with my clients is enough for me to jumpstart their progress. Once they're consistently seeing progress, their mind shifts to wanting to eat healthy in order to keep the progress going.

Baby steps can be the best steps.

Once you have identified what your top priorities are for self-improvement, you can then start planning your process for accomplishing your top goals. Part 3 – Setting Goals, discussed in detail how to successfully create achievable goals. Setting SMART goals, both short-term and long-term, makes up the bulk of planning ahead. Identifying and reaching out to your support system is another part to planning. Not to mention, the time invested in educating yourself about your goal prior to starting.

To illustrate, if you want to start doing a keto diet, it's important to research – using reliable sources – what it takes for your body to get into ketosis and how to transition your body from using carbohydrates as its primary energy source to fats. Understanding the proper way of doing this kind of nutrition plan involves consuming *healthy* fats, and it's not an excuse to only eat bacon, cheese, pork rinds, sausage, butter, etc. Such education also involves learning that the amount of electrolytes consumed while in ketosis is significantly reduced. It's crucial to monitor your sodium, magnesium, calcium, and potassium levels, as well as daily fiber intake.

The key aspect of planning, and the focal point of the example, is to gather as much information as possible to ensure the successful achievement of your desired goals.

Once you've decided on goals that are deeply meaningful to you, it's important to then create rituals – actions that follow a form, order, and frequency. Rituals can also be described as routines.

For example, it is impossible to get fit by working out once. Wouldn't that save us a lot of time! But, instead, we have to create a schedule where we work out on a consistent basis in order to achieve our goals.

The rituals will be different for everyone; this variance includes the content, frequency, length, and so forth. All of this is revealed when we plan ahead.

Once you have all of the details down, and you've started working on your goals, it is extremely important for you to stay organized. This will depend on your goal. Maybe this involves keeping track of every workout: what you did, how much weight you used, how you felt, or even setting out your workout clothes the night before so you don't have to think about it in the morning, etc. If your goal is nutrition-focused, maybe organization involves writing down everything you eat, portion sizes, body feedback, staying on top of going to the grocery store, and prepping foods before you run out, etc. If you're aiming to increase your daily water intake, you might need to organize details such as quantity, assessable water sources, bathrooms locations, and setting reminders on your smartphone to ensure regular hydration.

Every goal will require maintaining organization throughout the process so that you can stay on track. This is vital for success.

Self-Discovery: Planning Promotes Progress

Review your regular daily schedule (ideally for one entire week). Put down every detail. Break down every hour of your normal, everyday routines onto some type of calendar or list. This could be a sheet of paper where you draw the lines for the week. It could be a digital calendar. Do whatever works the best for you.

For the people who are planners and organizers, this will be fun! For everyone else – the people who like to "fly by the seat of their pants" and the procrastinators – just remember that this step will create success! Allowing yourself the opportunity to cultivate success is a demonstration of self-love.

Break things down to the smallest increments you can, within reason. I'm not saying you need to plan *every minute*, but at minimum, plan every hour; every thirty-minute segment is a phenomenal block of time to focus on.

Sometimes, it can help if you write down how long each task will take. Estimation is fine, and you can adjust as needed.

Keep pressing on until you believe everything in your average week is accounted for. Having this visual will create clarity and help you stay focused every day.

Then, plan out the times for your new goals: a fitness schedule, healthy meal preparation, shopping for healthy food items, or whatever you need to do to achieve your weekly goals. Write it down and/or add it to your calendar.

If you are engaging in this exercise, I am super-proud of you for working on setting yourself up for success! High-five!

Next, we will reimagine the process of losing weight. When you find your passion, you find your way.

Find Your Passion

"If you can't figure out your purpose, figure out your passion. For your passion will lead you right into your purpose." — Bishop T.D. Jakes

Most of us have heard the phrase, "Do what you love, and you'll never work another day in your life."

It essentially means that when you're doing something you truly love to do, even if you have to work from 9 to 5, midnight to 8am, or with coworkers who aren't that friendly, the job won't feel like work. It will bring you joy.

That doesn't mean that every day is going to be easy or that you're going to love doing every task associated with that job.

Deep down, the underlying meaning of the phrase is this: When you're following your passion, even those difficult days, the deadlines, the mistakes, or unmet expectations won't weigh as heavily on you; adversity won't have a profound impact.

More importantly, you will have a strong desire to embrace the challenging days and keep giving as much effort as possible because it is deeply meaningful to you.

My true purpose would never have been revealed if I'd avoided challenging times. The strength within me was uncovered through personal struggles and adversity. It was through healing my mind, body, and spirit that I discovered my passion and potential for helping others. And there is absolutely nothing more deeply meaningful to me than helping others. Nothing.

Now, every day, I am blessed to help guide others toward reviving their lives by regaining control, helping them discover their purpose and passions for living a healthy lifestyle that will have a ripple effect for everyone they know and meet. Discovering all of the dimensions of who I am today took time, but it created confidence and comfort, knowing that I am truly where I should be.

If I can help even just one person with this book, I know it will have been a success. Trust me when I say that discovering what is meaningful to you is worth the effort; otherwise, you risk settling for a less fulfilling life.

Most people, unfortunately, do not follow their passions in life. That's because people barely take the time required to figure out what their passions are.

Specifically, when it comes to one's career, people may follow the advice of parents, teachers, friends, and anyone else who tells them what they should or shouldn't be doing.

Whether we decide to go to college or not, some of us decide what our career path will be as we're finishing high school; around the ages of seventeen or eighteen. As we mature and age, what is important to us may change – such a shift is very common, in fact.

Early in life, we start focusing on a career that we have some interest in or relates to something we think we're good at. Then, along the way, we begin to lose that passion because it evolves into something else. A lot of young adults complete their education for what they think is their passion, and then, as soon as they're on the job, they realize their day-to-day tasks do not bring them joy or fulfillment.

When it comes to finding our passion for getting healthy, there are many obstacles in our modern lives. Oddly enough, as busy as most people think they are, the vast majority of them have a tendency to live sedentary lives. In previous generations, people had to be physically active just to survive. They worked on farms, in factories, in mills, or doing other jobs to pay the bills, and that activity burned a lot of energy. They burned a tremendous number of calories.

In modern society, most of us have sedentary jobs requiring very little physical activity. You might sit at a desk for eight, nine, or ten hours a day, getting little opportunity to stretch, move around, and exercise. That's why staying active is so important – because, as we get older, most of us become more sedentary. We must find ways to keep moving if our job lacks in that department.

A lot of us are also mentally worn out and exhausted, and have little energy left in the day to pursue our passions. So, we fill the void with other things, whether that's watching TV, being on social media for far longer than we've intended, snacking, indulging in "therapeutic" chocolate, consuming high-sugar drinks, or drinking more alcoholic beverages than recommended by the American Heart Association.

Most of these vices are symptoms of a person who's not fulfilling their real passion or purpose. Because, if we were fulfilling our purpose and passion, our daily routines would be different.

While I didn't write this book with the intention of helping you uncover the secrets of your life and transform every aspect of it, there are many crossover points between your passion and purpose in life, and your desire to live a healthy lifestyle.

There may very well be obstacles still in your way that prevent you from changing your career, moving from a job you are completely miserable into doing something you love. Just because those obstacles exist, though, does not mean you cannot begin mapping out a plan to change the course of your life now.

At this moment, though, you are here, reading this book because you have a desire to get healthy, have more energy, feel good in your own skin again, be stronger mentally and physically, and/or become a great role model for someone you care about.

Ultimately, the journey to discovering and following your passion is not only about finding joy in your daily tasks but also about navigating through challenges and unexpected turns. Embracing the difficult days with determination and effort becomes more meaningful when aligned with your true purpose. The pursuit of your passions is worth the effort, offering a path to fulfillment that transcends a settled life.

Now is the moment to start mapping out a plan for change, aligning your health goals with your deeper passions and purpose. As you read this book, driven by your desire for health and well-being, remember that this journey is a powerful catalyst for broader positive transformations in your life.

No Gym Membership Required

Many people immediately assume, when I start talking about fitness, that they have to join a gym.

You don't. In fact, going out and purchasing a gym membership before you have any plan in place could be a recipe for failure.

Why?

To be honest, going out and buying a gym membership without a plan is often a sign of external motivation. There are other things you need to establish and acknowledge first, such as:

- That you are focused on getting fit.

- That you understand the types of exercise optimal for you.
- That you're learning how to ease your way into it rather than doing too much too soon and burning out.
- That you've studied how to stay injury-free
- That you have decided whether going to the gym fits into your schedule.
- That you know who's going to watch your kids while you're at the gym.

Once you've taken steps such as these, *then* a gym membership makes sense. Like I mentioned, planning ahead promotes progress!

Too often, though, a person doesn't have a passion for going to the gym. They feel compelled. They have this extrinsic motivation tied to it, which means they're doing it for some other reason besides themselves or their driving purpose.

On the flip side of the same coin, you have many people (maybe even you yourself) who avoid gym memberships because they don't like working out, they feel intimidated, they have this idea that people are staring at them, or maybe they don't like the idea of using a machine that somebody else has sweated all over.

Whatever has motivated you to get a gym membership that you've never used or to avoid gyms altogether, understand that gyms are not a necessary component or the only way to become physically active or lose weight.

Yes, I advocate staying fit through physical activity and focusing on nutrition, but I want you to understand that a *gym membership is not necessary* for you to get in shape and become healthy.

Instead, you need to find your passion when it comes to physical activity. There are many ways you can get exercise – and even work out all of your body's muscle groups – without using those fancy machines at your local gym.

If you have a passion for some type of physical activity, that's a great starting point. Maybe you love swimming. Great! I also encourage you to try different things that might interest you – things you always wanted to do, but never pursued.

Think outside of the box. *Get creative!* You might find that you absolutely love skiing, snowboarding, paddleboarding, kayaking, hiking, gardening, or even cleaning the house! Now, I know the last one isn't usually that much fun, but most people have no idea how many calories they are burning simply by cleaning their home.

I used to clean my parents' house for them once a month. I would spend 7-8 hours cleaning with a 30-45-minute lunch break in the middle of the day. And I would typically burn between 1,000 and 1,250 calories each time I cleaned!

Now, I realize all day is a long time to spend cleaning; not everyone has that time. But imagine if you simply cleaned your house for a half a day: major calories burned and a clean house! WIN, WIN!

I know a lot of folks who hire someone else to clean their home. Here's my two cents: Don't pay someone to do it for you when you could save that money and incorporate some low impact exercise. I love cleaning. It's very relaxing for me. And the amazing thing is that cleaning house is such a light form of exercise, it doesn't seem like you're burning that many calories, but you are.

And, while I'm on the subject of cleaning, what about washing your automobile? There's another calorie-burning option we take for granted. By doing these chores, you're burning calories, but also boosting your morale, productivity, strengthening your work ethic, and your sense of accomplishment.

Oh, and let's not forget SEX! Oh, yes. Let's not be shy now. This is a calorie-burning activity ... *and* a relationship-builder. See? We're multitasking. I'm sure your partner will agree that sexercise is an excellent idea!

In 2013, a research study assessed the calorie consumption during sexual activity among young, healthy couples in their everyday setting and compared it with a session of endurance exercise. The study revealed that men burn an average of 4.2 calories per minute (approx. 101 calories total) during sex, while women burn approximately 3.1 calories per minute (approx. 69 calories total).[50] During multiple studies regarding heart rate during sex, the average heart rate ranged from 90 to 130 beats per minute. Peak heart rate ranged from 145 to 170 beats per minute.[51]

There are many variables to these statistics, of course, including the overall health metrics of the participants, duration (studies found that the average duration was twenty minutes), which partner exerts more effort, and so forth. But the case remains: Engaging in sexual activity could be regarded as a substantial form of physical activity under the right circumstances.

But, unless you are engaging in sexual activity quite often, though, you most likely will not see weight loss as a direct reflection of your sexual activity alone.

Keep in mind, engaging in sexual activity has also been associated with stress reduction, enhanced mental well-being, decreased risk of heart attacks, and increased longevity.

If you need more ideas for different types of fitness goals, or events, to work toward, here are some ideas:

- Spartan races
- Bicycle races

- Triathlons
- Relay events
- 5k, 10k, 50k, 90k runs
- Mountain Hikes

There are even races where you get to eat doughnuts or drink beer! (This is totally counterproductive, but the races are out there!) Also, many events support a cause or foundation. If the idea of supporting something good gets you moving, I say, "Do it!"

How do you begin?

You need to tap into your passion. When you manage to do this, you will be able to keep pushing when you are in that initial phase – the stage that is the hardest and tests you the most. Staying consistent and determined will ensure success and even enjoyment in the process.

On the next page, the infographic from Live Science gives examples of calorie expenditures for different activities based on 30-minute intervals, for individuals weighing 164 lb. and 196 lb.

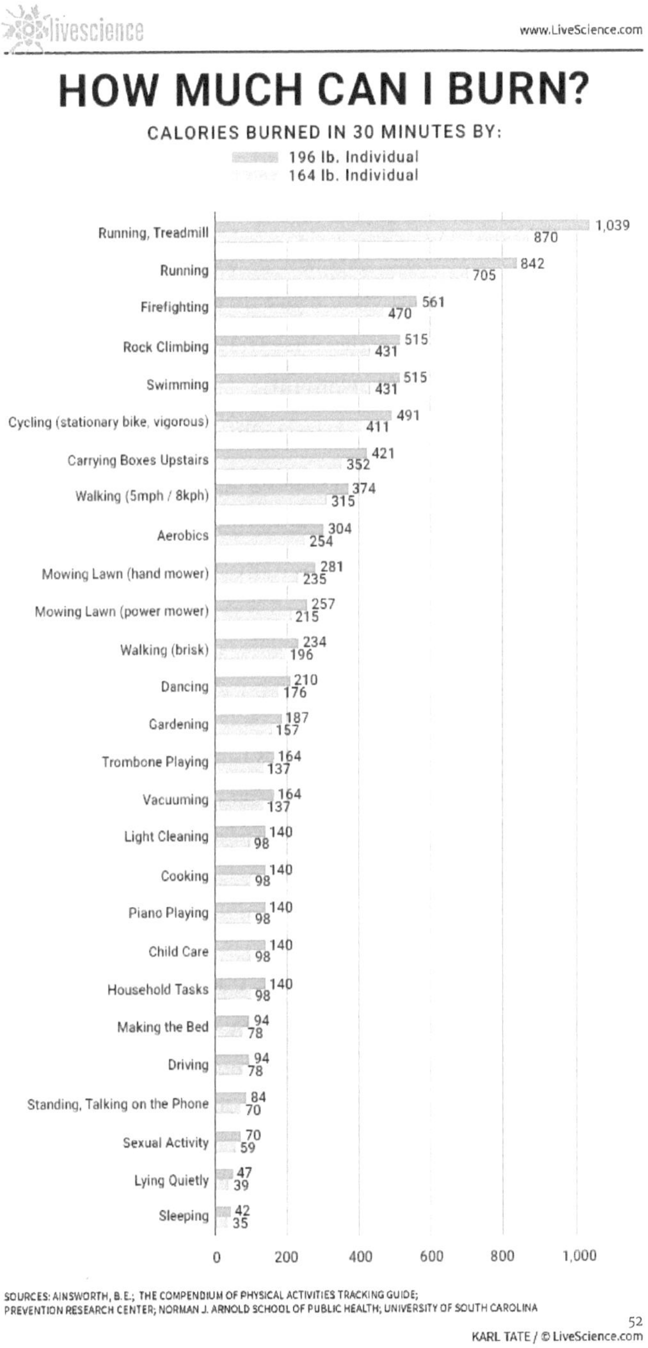
livescience
www.LiveScience.com
HOW MUCH CAN I BURN?
CALORIES BURNED IN 30 MINUTES BY:
196 lb. Individual
164 lb. Individual
Running, Treadmill 1,039 870
Running 842 705
Firefighting 561 470
Rock Climbing 515 431
Swimming 515 431
Cycling (stationary bike, vigorous) 491 411
Carrying Boxes Upstairs 421 352
Walking (5mph / 8kph) 374 315
Aerobics 304 254
Mowing Lawn (hand mower) 281 235
Mowing Lawn (power mower) 257 215
Walking (brisk) 234 196
Dancing 210 176
Gardening 187 157
Trombone Playing 164 137
Vacuuming 164 137
Light Cleaning 140 98
Cooking 140 98
Piano Playing 140 98
Child Care 140 98
Household Tasks 140 98
Making the Bed 94 78
Driving 94 78
Standing, Talking on the Phone 84 70
Sexual Activity 70 59
Lying Quietly 47 39
Sleeping 42 35
0
200
400
600
800
1,000
SOURCES: AINSWORTH, B.E.; THE COMPENDIUM OF PHYSICAL ACTIVITIES TRACKING GUIDE; PREVENTION RESEARCH CENTER; NORMAN J. ARNOLD SCHOOL OF PUBLIC HEALTH; UNIVERSITY OF SOUTH CAROLINA
KARL TATE / © LiveScience.com

52

Meet Morgan

Morgan was an extremely active person when I met her. She was a straight shooter, served in the military, and had an endearing sense of humor. Morgan also loved being outdoors. When we met, she was in her mid-40s and had a son whom she loved more than anything else.

Morgan joined my group fitness classes on a regular basis. She was crushing her workouts, but I got the sense that she was frustrated, and maybe even bored with some of the circuits.

One day after class, I decided to discuss this impression with her. What I discovered was that her passion was in doing physically strenuous activities outdoors, not confined to a room. Indoors, she found herself losing motivation, which was unintentionally reducing the intensity of her workouts.

What really spoke to her were activities such as mountain biking, paddle boarding, and trail running. These seemed to be her favorites, but she had a long list of physical activities that included being amongst nature. After she recounted some of those desires, I asked her why she wasn't doing these activities more often and why she was focusing on activities that weren't providing her with any real emotional fulfillment.

The danger in focusing on certain activities that you're not inspired to do or working out in an environment you're not enjoying is that typically you will eventually find excuses to avoid those activities.

But, I found that Morgan had plenty of excuses that helped her rationalize why she couldn't do the activities that *were* more enjoyable to her, including things like, "What if it's too cold outside?" and "What if it's raining?"

Given enough contemplation, one can rapidly conjure a myriad of excuses to entirely sidestep the opportunity of exercising. Yet, even in the midst of excuses, there are options and alternatives.

Sure, Morgan enjoyed being outside rather than indoors, but she was worried about what to do when the weather wouldn't cooperate. The solution was simple. When it rained, she could go to the gym and get in a great workout. When the weather was cooperating, she could take advantage of it.

Sometimes, our minds go to a place of all or nothing. But if you're passionate about doing something, *you* are truly the only one who can make it happen.

For Morgan, when it was cold out, dressing appropriately by bundling up was doable. On exceptionally cold or rainy days, she could go to the gym or workout at home to complete her exercises.

She also expressed that there were certain days when she simply couldn't go outdoors because of her work schedule, her son's school activities, or other things going on in her life. I advised her to switch the days of her workouts so that she could get outside more often. For instance, she might choose to forgo exercise on her busiest days, such as workdays her son has after-school activities.

Together, we worked on a schedule that made sense not just for her life, but for her passions of being outdoors and doing the activities that brought her joy.

I saw Morgan less and less in my group fitness classes, and that was perfectly fine. She and I stayed in connection outside of the gym, and she explained that she was staying in shape through other external means. Her son was even starting to do some of those activities with her, too.

You see, there's that common theme coming together again: Our children and other people we care about will see us, be inspired by us, and may even join us in our adventures.

Depending on where you live, though, it may be nearly impossible to get creative with some of the ways you can exercise. Take time to consider things like location and weather as you decide on the best options *for you.*

Takeaways from Morgan

It truly doesn't matter how you choose to burn your calories. Having a passion for improving your health is an excellent starting point. However, when your exercise routines start feeling dull, repetitive, or uninspiring, it's time to explore physical activities that truly ignite your personal passion.

Look for activities that genuinely interest you and get creative! If you find it challenging due to your location or other factors, don't hesitate to reach out to me for a free one-on-one consultation. You'll soon realize that numerous opportunities are available to you. The crucial thing is to persevere and not give up if you're facing this particular roadblock.

Remember, the path to a healthier lifestyle is unique to each individual, and finding activities you genuinely enjoy can make the journey more enjoyable and sustainable. So, whether it's a scenic hike, a dance class, or a virtual workout routine, embrace the variety available to you and remember that each step you take is a positive stride toward achieving your health and fitness goals.

Furthermore, it's about making your health journey not just a routine but an enjoyable part of your lifestyle.

The key is resilience. By staying determined and seeking out activities that excite you, you're not only overcoming challenges but also nurturing a sustainable and fulfilling approach to your well-being.

Keep the momentum going, and you'll find that the journey itself becomes a rewarding and empowering part of your life.

Self-Discovery: What Are Your Passions?

Maybe you've never really been a physically active person. That's okay. I don't want you to worry about that.

What I want you to think about are the things you might have once had an interest in pursuing, or still do have an interest in, even if you've never participated in them up to this point.

Was there a time when you thought about going hiking or kayaking, or doing yoga, gardening, or playing tennis?

There are endless activities you can do on your own or even join a group so that you and others can encourage one another.

Earlier in this book, I had you self-reflect about activities you currently do and that would realistically align with your schedule. Now let's dive even deeper into creating a list of physical activities that you are truly passionate about and that aid in losing weight.

First off, answer this question: What type of "athlete" are you?

There's no wrong answer here. If you've never been athletic in your life, that doesn't mean you don't have the potential to excel at something. You may have tried different things growing up or as an adult. What have you dabbled in that you feel you were good at or loved doing? Is there something you have never tried, but always wanted to? What are you passionate about? These should all be things you are passionate about.

Take a moment to self-reflect and think about it. If you were once involved in any sport activities, such as in high school or college, what were they? Are you still athletic in that sport? Is it something you'd like to do again?

After contemplating this, I want you to prioritize your list in terms of the options you are most passionate about at the top. If you find your list is empty or only has one option, keep reflecting on the questions asked. These need to be physical activities, whether gardening, jogging, yoga, kayaking, or anything else.

With each of the physical activities you've prioritized, I want you to write down the what, when, how, and where. For example, *what* am I doing? *What* do I need to do to execute this? *When* am I doing it? *What* day of the week and *what* time of day? *How* am I going to plan ahead and prepare so I can successfully do it? *Where* does it take place? Also, am I doing it with someone or on my own?

Feel free to add your own questions to answer.

Lastly, write down *why* you are passionate about this and want to do it, or why you liked doing it in the past.

You should now have a short list of physical activities you can do, and are passionate about, that will help you lose weight. It is wonderful when you can enjoy doing the things you love!

Because these are personal interests, you will enjoy doing these things on a regular basis and therefore be more likely to maintain consistency. Doing physical activities you look forward to is a far greater motivator than forcing yourself to do them for the sake of health. Focus on physical activities you enjoy. This way, you'll stay passionate about becoming fit!

Learn Tenaciously

"The capacity to learn is a gift; the ability to learn is a skill; the willingness to learn is a choice." — Brian Herbert

It's no secret that we live in an incredibly busy world. There are so many distractions, but there are also tremendous responsibilities. It seems that the more technology we have (*supposedly* designed to simplify life), the faster life moves.

We have emails, text messages, and alerts constantly flooding our minds, many of them needing responses. There are more and more advertisements grabbing our attention to distract us.

To be truly productive and have an efficient day, we *must* prioritize. But the top priority for everyone – no matter whether you are a high-level executive, an entrepreneur, a stay-at-home mom, a teacher, a nurse, or anything else – is your *health.*

Nothing else even comes close.

Unfortunately, most of us place our health as a lower priority. We avoid that visit to the doctor's office for our preventative care appointments. We tend not to eat healthy meals like we know we should, simply because our health seems fine now. We neglect to consider the long-term consequences of our actions. Too many of us adopt unhealthy habits as a way to cope with the stressors we face, and over time, these habits have the potential to create more future dilemmas.

The American Heart Association has revealed that around 436,852 individuals in the United States succumb to sudden cardiac arrest annually.[53] As per the World Health Organization, cardiovascular ailments like heart attacks and strokes rank as the primary cause of mortality – accounting for a staggering 17.9 million deaths each year worldwide, constituting 31% of all fatalities.[54] Cardiovascular diseases encompass a range of disorders impacting the heart and blood vessels. Various factors can contribute to their development, including elevated blood pressure, high cholesterol, tobacco consumption, poor dietary choices, lack of physical activity, and obesity. This is mainly due to neglecting our health. Such behavior is a slippery slope because, the more we stay sedentary, the more our bodies want to stay that way. Your body will always want to stay where it is the most comfortable. So, if you allow your mind to rationalize why it's okay to move less, it will. But a body in motion will always find a way to stay in motion.

As we get older, our family dynamic changes. We usually get married, potentially have children, and then, as we move through our 30s, 40s, and 50s, our health should become an even higher priority. Why? Because time catches up with us. Unhealthy decisions catch up with us. The choices we've made in our 20s and 30s will carry into our 40s and 50s.

But if you have been diagnosed with cancer, like I have, what becomes the priority?

Your health becomes the priority.

The crucial point is that your health should *always* take precedence – not just when things are going south and you're dealing with an ailment. Yet, unless there's a serious health emergency, our personal health tends to sit lower on our priority list, getting less attention than our spouses, children, careers, and other responsibilities.

This lack of prioritization is one of the main reasons so many people don't seek out expert guidance on their nutrition, fitness, and overall health. This is why so many people fail to visit the doctor as often as they should. It's also why some folks don't go to the dentist until their teeth start hurting. Certainly, there are additional reasons, but neglecting to prioritize such matters is a significant factor.

In this mindset, health is not a priority.

The best way to understand your priorities is by gathering information. When you gather information, you can convert it to knowledge. Often, we think of information as knowledge, but that's not the case. Information is just that: information.

Full comprehension means having a complete understanding of what we're learning and how to apply it properly. That's when information is converted into knowledge. You can have all of the information in the world about healthy nutrition, or the most efficient exercise regimens, but if you don't completely understand it, it's not really knowledge.

Knowledge gives you power.

The more you know, the more you prioritize. And if you have all this knowledge, but you do nothing with it, what's the point of learning it in the first place?

To sustain a healthy lifestyle, it's important to take the time to research the right options for *you*, understand your newfound knowledge, and begin applying it to your daily life. This is how you create a sense of personal power and gain control of your life.

It's also important to learn with a skeptical eye. I advise you to have your information stem from published scientific journals, research studies, and credible experts with the appropriate knowledge, experience, and ability to decipher fact from fiction.

The internet can be tricky. While in your favorite search engine, skip any search results labeled as advertisement. These are companies paying to promote themselves, ensuring they appear at the top of your search results. It is a common best practice to avoid advertisements. Also, try to steer clear of any mainstream media websites, as they are typically biased and may only promote their sponsors' products. Additionally, check for factors such as whether the website is an unbiased source, if the information is presented objectively or subjectively, if independent studies are conducted, if the source adheres to industry standards, and if the website allows anyone to add information, making it unreliable, and so forth.

Navigating social media can be particularly challenging due to its open nature. The platform allows virtually anyone to share content without necessarily demonstrating expertise in a given topic. In this vast sea of information, it is crucial for users to exercise discernment and conduct thorough research on individuals or companies behind the content in which they are learning from and researching.

Given the free nature of social media, where voices from various backgrounds can be heard, misinformation or content lacking credibility can easily find its way onto your feed. Therefore, I encourage you to double check the credentials of anyone sharing content and assess the reliability of the sources they cite.

In addition, make sure to research the pros and cons of your subject matter. What are people saying who are "for" or "against" it, and why?

When you have information from both sides, then you can make an informed decision that's right for you.

Mentorship

Striving for your health goals can absolutely be done on your own. I have no doubt about that. However, when it comes to nutrition, exercise, stress management, properly implementing healthy habits, and balancing your hormones, a professional will take all of the guesswork out of the equation.

Seek out professional, experienced assistance where appropriate. Working with a mentor is a proven process for success. This might be something you have to invest in, but you will save money in the long run. You will actually spend more time and money trying to "wing it" yourself than if you locate a mentor and achieve the progress you desire with a faster timeline.

A mentor can be a professional who has the knowledge and experience you desire, but it can also be an experienced person who's already achieved the goal you're striving for. This doesn't guarantee you'll share the same results, but it could be a good option to try.

Search online or locally to find potential mentors. Interview them, or simply chat, to find out if they are the right fit for you and if they are willing to be your mentor.

Explain to them what your vision and mission are and specify the type of advice you are seeking. Ensure that your mentorship is structured, with regular meetings and a clear agenda.

There is no reason to reinvent the wheel or make mistakes that other people have already made. With an open mind, allow a mentor to help guide you to faster results.

Meet Kasey

When I met her, Kasey was generally quite social, a woman who loved to be around people. She was incredibly friendly, charming, and inquisitive. She loved learning.

And she was the kind of person who, when you met her, you couldn't help but be inspired to learn like she was learning. There was a wealth of information at her disposal, and she was constantly taking advantage of that and trying to improve.

She was a mother of two teenagers, and she was in her late 40s. I was coaching at a small, niche gym when we met.

I sat down with Kasey, and we discussed her weight loss goals, the obstacles challenging her, and her next action steps. She didn't need a lot of guidance; Kasey had most things well under control.

She tended to be quite consistent with her exercise routines, and she was also making some wonderfully healthy food choices, but Kasey wanted more.

She didn't think she knew enough about fitness and nutrition. Kasey wanted to dive deeper into some of these exercises and know precisely which ones focused on which muscle groups.

The more we talked, the more I came to realize, and understand, that Kasey was most concerned about back exercises she could use to help strengthen her lumbar. Kasey also wanted to explore a new nutrition plan and recipes for her family that were healthy. She was determined to provide proper nutrition and help her family feel healthier and more energized.

Kasey was an incredibly driven person and wanted to learn more independently. She knew there was a wealth of information at her disposal thanks to the Internet, but she found it hard to decipher between the accurate information and the misleading content. Kasey was trying to be very cautious and careful about what she read and accepted. I started her off with a few tips about things she could do while conducting research. She could start by contacting her medical care provider, visiting her local library, or taking advantage of worldwide resources such as:

mayoclinic.com, medicalnewstoday.com, examine.com, apa.org, sciencedirect.com, healthline.com, or hopkinsmedicine.org.

To ensure a comprehensive understanding, it's crucial to leverage resources like these to examine information both in favor of and against your chosen topic.

The goal is not merely to seek confirmation of preconceived notions but to engage in thorough research, considering diverse perspectives and gathering a well-rounded comprehension of the subject. This approach contributes to a more nuanced and informed perspective, fostering critical thinking and a more accurate grasp of the complexities surrounding the topic at hand.

I also advised Kasey not to hesitate to reach out to me if she had any questions. As time went on, Kasey would randomly come to me, sharing the latest information she gathered – sometimes because she was excited about learning something new, and other times to confirm whether what she'd found was accurate or not. It was great to also receive text messages and images of the latest dinner recipe she was trying out. I was incredibly proud of the initiative she was taking, so I kept encouraging her.

Kasey was constantly learning and growing. This was empowering her, and she was inspiring *me* at the same time.

When you are constantly learning on your own, like Kasey was, you will feel just as empowered as she did. By actively learning, she was taking the information she gathered and applying it to her own life. When you apply intrigue and a passion toward any subject matter, the process will help keep you focused, curious, and seeking more information for the betterment of yourself. That is the best way to create lasting success!

Takeaways from Kasey

One of the extraordinary aspects of life is that there is never a time or place where we have to stop learning. Our experiences bring about changes that enable us to think and feel differently, and therefore compelling us to take different steps or follow a different path. There are many aspects to learning and growing as an individual.

Remember, you are *AMAZING!* Not just because you want to improve your life, get healthy, perhaps shed some weight, have more energy, or be a great role model for your children, spouse, or friends, but also because you are taking on an incredibly rewarding, yet challenging, path in life: prioritizing your health.

In addition, you are willing to learn something new. After all, what you have learned up to this point, and perhaps the habits you have developed, have not led you to the place you want to be, at least not in the physical and health sense.

Whatever your goals are in life, part of the path to creating success is understanding your goal *completely* by constantly learning more about your goal *and yourself.*

That involves asking important questions like:

- <u>What</u> is my goal?
- <u>Why</u> is this goal important to me?
- <u>How</u> do I achieve this?
- <u>What are the resources I need</u> to achieve this?
- <u>What are the pros and cons</u> to pursuing this venture?
- <u>When is it realistic</u> for me to achieve this?

When you start asking these questions, you dig deeper into your own mindset. When you are mentally ready to strive for what's truly meaningful to you, you'll be ready to commit to learning.

As I mentioned, information is readily available everywhere. Yet, most of us quickly forget the information we're exposed to. This is because we aren't connecting it to any real meaning or purpose in our current lives. It's just information.

But when it means something to you, when you have a sincere desire to understand that information, to absorb it, and to let it begin to positively change you as a person, then it becomes impactful.

When it came to researching about a specific health topic, Kasey never accepted the first answer she got. I would not want *you* to, either. Give yourself time to do the research in order to determine whether the information you have found is reliable and accurate. Understand your source's mission statement and check to make sure the company isn't simply promoting their own products or partnering with other companies and using their products.

It takes dedication and effort to uncover true, unbiased research. Understand the data by asking questions such as, "Who was the research funded by?" and "What was their focus?" Research the pros and cons of your subject matter, and then make an informed decision that is best for *you* and your situation. If you find that multiple sources are saying the same thing, that's usually an indicator that there's validity to your research findings.

If you have someone in the health industry whom you trust, don't hesitate to seek their professional advice.

I encourage my clients to turn to me if they have questions about any information they have uncovered, especially online. If I am not sure whether it's accurate, I will research it myself. Knowing where reliable information can be found helps clarify its accuracy and identifies whether there is any new or recently published information.

Try not to simply rely on what your friend, or your friend's friend, told you, or what you see on social media as gospel. Too often, it is inaccurate, fake, or designed to sell something.

If you see something that looks promising, take it with a grain of salt and then do diligent research. Remember, if it seems way too good to be true, it probably is.

But once you are armed with the knowledge you need, you will have the power to succeed!

Self-Discovery: Know Thyself

Without a clear understanding of what holds genuine importance to you in the present moment, initiating action and investing the necessary effort for positive change becomes considerably more challenging. That is the essence of what this book is about: helping you to understand yourself, your purpose, and your ultimate motivation for wanting to get healthy and sustain a healthy lifestyle.

Take time to write down and figure out all of the details about the aspects I outline below. Take your time with this. I encourage you to focus on this activity before moving on to the next section of this book.

These are not difficult questions, but they will help you dig deeper and narrow down the best process for you moving forward.

If your goals pertain to something else other than exercising and eating healthy, simply modify these questions to appropriately address your specific goals.

- What is your plan for increasing your physical activity?
- Is this the best course of action for you right now?
    - If so, how can this plan create success?
    - If not, what is Plan B?
- What do you need to facilitate this properly?
    - Will you have access to your resources as needed?
- Does your plan have an overarching outcome-based goal as well as smaller milestone behavior-based goals?
- Have you given yourself a realistic time frame?
- How do you plan to stay accountable?
- With all honesty, how motivated are you to get started and start implementing this plan?
- What is your plan for improving your nutrition?
- Is this the best course of action for you right now?
    - If so, how can this plan create success?
    - If not, what is Plan B?
- What do you need to facilitate this properly?
    - Will you have access to your resources as needed?
- Does your plan have an overarching outcome-based goal as well as smaller milestone behavior-based goals?
- Have you given yourself a realistic time frame?
- How do you plan to stay accountable?
- How motivated are you to start implementing this plan?

<u>What Works Best for Your Body?</u>

Questions to ask regarding your plan for workouts and food choices you plan to select:

- Has this worked for your body in the past?

- Has this created optimal results before?
- If you're unsure, why have you chosen these options?
- Are your plans flexible if you need to modify?

Understanding what works best for your body may include needing to modifying your workout schedule, the exercises you do, the types of food choices you consume, the number of meals or snacks you have each day, and so forth. The more flexible your game plan is, the easier it will be for you to stick to it. The more rigid you are with yourself, the harder it will be. Keep experimenting until you discover the most ideal strategies for what *your* body needs to excel.

If you have a medical condition, research every aspect of it before exercising and/or changing your eating habits.

I recommend discussing your new, independent health plan with your doctor. There is no excuse for not playing it safe. When it comes to your medical history and health, *always* consult your doctor if you have any questions or concerns. This will include any new, old, chronic health issues, pain management that you are dealing with, injuries, recovering from surgery, etc. It's vital that you understand any ailment you may have. Research every detail you can about it—what it is, the symptoms it can cause, and how it affects you. Discover whether or not there are workarounds or modifications. Can you adjust behaviors, habits, or your daily routine, such as by making sure the chair you sit in for eight hours a day at work is ergonomically correct, or perhaps adding stretching to your daily schedule?

If you are taking any medications (prescription or over-the-counter), understand the potential side effects, things to stay away from while using the medication(s), and anything you *should* be doing while taking any medications.

Just like Kasey, you can transform your life for the better with a little due diligence, going through each day, learning, and growing.

Never Give Up!

"Do not fear failure but rather fear not trying." — Roy T. Bennett

There was a sci-fi comedy in the late '90s called *Galaxy Quest*. The big celebrities who starred in it were Tim Allen and Sigourney Weaver. The show was about a bunch of *Star Trek*-type, second-rate actors getting caught up in an actual intergalactic war where the beings had a simple saying: *Never give up; never surrender.*

Even in the face of overwhelming odds, complete and utter defeat, that's the one thing their devoted leader continued to say.

You can find a plethora of quotes about never giving up:

- *"Winners never quit, and quitters never win." — Vince Lombardi*
- *"Never give up on something that you can't go a day without thinking about." — Winston Churchill*

These are wonderful quotes and reminders about the importance of perseverance. At the heart of them is: Never give up.

At this point, we have discussed everything you need to create true, lasting success with your health goals and priorities. However, there's one last piece of the proverbial puzzle that we cannot overlook.

That's right, you guessed it: Never give up.

Incorporating new, healthy habits into your busy life and daily routine is hard! This isn't simply an opinion. It's a common consensus. If you feel this way, let me tell you flat-out, "You are *not* alone."

Let me repeat that:

You. Are. Not. Alone.

No matter what type of change you are pursuing, long-lasting change is going to require conscious effort on your part, at least in the beginning. Fortunately, this is only temporary.

Once you push through the most difficult aspects of this type of change in your life (the first 2-4 weeks), the level of conscious effort will start to decrease. You may need to remind yourself every other day, a couple of times a week or once a week, and then eventually less often.

We need to remember this, especially in the beginning. Things *will* get easier. I promise.

There are innumerable stories about men and women who've faced incredible odds, challenges that would have crushed most of us in their wake, but despite all of that, *they had a belief in themselves, were driven by a meaningful purpose, and achieved what they believed was achievable.*

Look at the Space Race of the 1960s as a simple example. When President Kennedy announced that the U.S. would land a man on the moon by the end of the decade and then return him safely to the Earth, it was almost laughable. It was something from a sci-fi movie of that time. Yet, he and the greatest minds at NASA believed it was possible.

That did not mean success was easy. In fact, there was heartbreak along the way. There was tragedy. There was loss of life. There was defeat. And there were moments when some of those same leaders at NASA began to question if it was ever going to happen. Not just by the end of the decade, but ever. There were *many* obstacles.

This is only one example, but the point is simple: Never give up.

When it comes to your health goals, yes, there will be challenges. Yet, it is also incredibly rewarding to push through the pain, the doubt, the discomfort, the mistakes, the missed opportunities, and the defeats, and come out victorious in the end.

I can humbly say that I've never been someone who faced insurmountable odds or felt like the cards were stacked against me. But, I have survived through tough times, as we all have. At 29, I had the early stages of cervical cancer, but it was caught early enough that one surgery was the proper remedy. I've also experienced the most insane three months of my life while training for a competition, which I would never recommend for anyone. And in a commonality we all share, I have lost loved ones, and grief stills brings emotions of love and despair all at once when I think about them. I've been through a divorce, and no one ever wins there. It's simply a sad situation that you never imagine yourself being a part of. And, by a certain age, most of us have been hurt, betrayed, taken advantage of, lied to, and wronged.

But, personally, I wouldn't change any of my experiences for anything. When I reflect on all of the challenges I've faced up until this point, I truly feel blessed. The first thought that enters my mind is that all of these challenges have made me the strong, driven person who I am today. I am proud to be who I am today, and proud of the knowledge I've attained through the tough times.

I am perfectly imperfect. Each day is a miracle and a blessing, and I refuse to give up on anything in life, especially on myself.

One of the main reasons many people ultimately give up on their goals of positively transforming their lives – whether it's getting fit, changing eating habits, starting a new career, moving to a new place, or even battling an addiction – is that they simply give up on themselves.

The many people that start new habits don't always give their full effort, or they don't give their full effort *long enough* to successfully transition beyond the initial uncomfortable phase and into one of routine and relative ease.

They start "sprinting up the mountain" of their goal, but then get worn out. They don't pace themselves, and they get frustrated. There is a reason the overwhelming majority of people who try to reach the summit of Mount Everest fall short. It's not because they didn't really want to. After all, if you have to spend $30,000 (at a minimum) just to try, you're going to give it your best effort. No, the reason many people fall short is that they may start out by giving it their all, but then their mindset changes once the conditions become more challenging.

When it comes to living a healthy lifestyle, too many people give up on themselves before they reach the "top of the hill." They never conceptualize how breathtaking and glorious the summit is, where achievement and success exist and everything becomes easier, more routine, and they're feeling amazing. Instead, they looked up in the midst of feeling exhausted after a short while, just to see how far they still had to go. Then, they begin to feel defeated because they reflect on what's still ahead rather than on what they have accomplished. Not seeing the summit can make it feel even more out of reach, or even potentially impossible.

When your mantra is *Never give up; never surrender*, this simply means that you don't have to see the summit to continue putting one foot in front of the other. Yes, your muscles may burn, your joints may ache, and your body might experience pain, but all it takes is *just one more step*, then one more, and on you go.

In time, your body, mind, and spirit will be joined together in this routine of continually moving toward these amazing goals.

You *are* amazing simply because you started this journey. But starting the journey is not the end. It is not the destination.

New Habits Take Time

Forging new habits is a gradual and transformative process that requires both time and patience. It begins with acknowledging and letting go of unhealthy habits and behavioral patterns that have brought you to where you are today – feeling unsatisfied, but ready for change. If you've read this far, you're ready for change.

To cultivate new, healthy habits, patience becomes an essential virtue. Your guiding principle should be prioritizing *progress over perfection* because it's crucial to recognize that sustainable change takes time. Expecting immediate results can lead to frustration and many missed opportunities.

Consider this journey as a marathon rather than a sprint. Each step forward, no matter how small, contributes to your overall progress. Embrace the gradual nature of habit formation, understanding that consistency and persistence are key. Celebrate the small victories along the way, and view setbacks as learning opportunities and for adjusting.

In essence, transforming your habits is a holistic journey that involves self-reflection, commitment, and a recognition that true change takes time. By embracing patience and appreciating the progress you make along the way, you position yourself for sustainable success while on your quest for a healthier, more fulfilling lifestyle.

Work Hard

Transforming one's life is an incredible task, routines and habits are deeply embedded in the psyche. You cannot change everything right away — it takes time, and it definitely takes effort.

While adjusting dietary choices may appear straightforward in theory, the practical challenge becomes apparent when confronting longstanding patterns that have shaped one's lifestyle over the course of years. This endeavor demands a considerable amount of willpower and persistence, which is why making such a change must be deeply meaningful to you.

However, when you properly set yourself up for success with unwavering tenacity and determination, *you will get there*. Recognizing this process as a long-term investment rather than an instantaneous fix is crucial. By approaching the journey with diligence and resilience, one positions oneself for sustainable success in breaking free from ingrained habits and realizing meaningful change.

Stay Positive

It's extremely easy for us to fall into the Negative Nancy state of mind. We're often our own worst critics.

However, positive thinking doesn't imply ignoring unpleasant situations. Instead, it involves approaching such situations in a more positive and constructive manner. It entails anticipating the best outcomes rather than the worst.

Positive thinking often originates from self-talk, which refers to the constant flow of thoughts in our conscious and subconscious minds. These automatic thoughts can be either positive or negative. Some self-talk is based on logic and reason, while other thoughts may arise from misconceptions resulting from a lack of information or preconceived notions about potential outcomes.

Researchers are exploring the impact of positive thinking and optimism on health. Some potential health benefits associated with positive thinking include:

- Extended lifespan
- Decreased prevalence of depression
- Reduced levels of distress and pain
- Enhanced resilience against illnesses
- Improved psychological and physical well-being
- Enhanced cardiovascular health
- Lowered risk of cardiovascular disease and stroke-related mortality
- Lowered risk of mortality from cancer, respiratory conditions, and internal infections
- Improved ability to cope during difficult times and potentially stressful situations[55]

The reasons behind the health benefits experienced by individuals who practice positive thinking are not fully understood. However, one hypothesis suggests that maintaining a positive outlook helps individuals cope more effectively with stressful situations, thereby reducing the negative impact of stress on their physical well-being.[55]

Another viewpoint suggests that positive and optimistic individuals generally adopt healthier lifestyles.[55] They engage in regular physical activity, follow nutritious regimens, and refrain from excessive smoking or alcohol consumption. A positive mindset encompasses positive thoughts, beliefs, values, and attitudes, which are crucial elements for overall well-being.

Here are some common recommendations for cultivating a healthy, positive mindset:

- Focus on your strengths
- Practice gratitude
- Focus on your positive attributes
- Practice self-compassion and self-care
- Redirect your focus
- Try meditation focused on love and kindness
- Set Goals with personal significance
- Acceptance for the uncontrollable
- Build a resilient spirit
- Create consciousness and mindfulness: Be present
- Live a life of integrity[56,57]

Now, let's get acquainted with an inspiring story about Mia, an individual who embodies the power of resiliency and positivity.

Meet Mia

One excellent example of success in overcoming obstacles can be found in Mia. She was an extremely gentle soul in her mid-50s when we met. Mia was always thinking of others first and she was a mother of three children.

As an extremely family-focused mom, she enjoyed staying active, including with her children. She focused on cooking wholesome meals, but she never felt as though she was sacrificing or depriving herself of anything. She had an active social life and the right attitude of pursuing progress, not perfection.

Mia understood, too, that permanent change doesn't simply happen overnight. She was positive, patient, and persistent. She never gave up.

What made Mia's story stand out to me was that she battled debilitating back pain from time to time. She would be in and out of the gym — days when I would see her on a regular basis and then not. She kept me updated on her status, and I offered my assistance if she needed it. Mia explained there were times when the slightest movement would create the most unspeakable pain. There were other times when she didn't notice any pain whatsoever. The first step in her move toward change was awareness that she couldn't live the rest of her life like this.

As we get older, we begin to accept certain types of pain, loss of energy or flexibility, and potentially adding new medications to our daily regimen, and we may think, "I guess this is how it is now." But that doesn't have to be the case. There are always options available.

Mia did not want to live the rest of her life *like this*. She recognized that she was the only one who had the power to take control of her life and do something about her debilitating back pain. Mia didn't yet know what the cause was, but she remained positive and hopeful. She knew there had to be a solution.

First, she had to discover what her options were. Could physical therapy help? What about chiropractic medicine? Were these treatments only temporary? What were the risks? Could there be any side effects from certain treatments?

She spent time looking into possible treatment options, which included massage therapy, acupuncture, physical therapy, chiropractic medicine, yoga, decompression therapy, and so on. She then began to try different options to figure out what worked best for her body.

Not just for her body, either – but also her lifestyle, her schedule, and her family.

Whenever she ventured into uncharted territory, she actively sought expert guidance to gain a deeper understanding of her circumstances.

Even though she tried various approaches along the way, nothing brought the lasting relief she was hoping for.

She eventually found the options that alleviated her pain the most. It turned out to be a combination of tactics and therapies, which included taking a short time off from work to focus on rehabilitation and recovery.

Sometimes, that's exactly what we have to do, especially when we're trying to achieve optimal, long-lasting health. You may need to remove yourself from one thing to improve yourself in another. That's okay. If your work will give you the opportunity, and you need recovery time from an ailment, injury, surgery, or other medical issue, take advantage of that opportunity if you can.

Mia stuck with this process for *months*. She went through numerous highs and lows. There were days, even entire weeks, when she didn't notice much progress, if any at all. She felt emotionally overwhelmed and wondered how she could ever continue living life like this.

Then, there were days when she felt like her pain was gone – rare occasions where she had no pain and was reminded of what her life had been like before lower back pain. Days when she felt powerful, as though she could take on the world!

As weeks progressed into months, her body *finally* started to respond. It was a long, painful, difficult road, but she was finally able to return to the gym and begin working out as she once had, adding therapeutic options to her weekly routine.

Most importantly, she started to feel like herself again.

There were many points along that path when she could have given up. Yet, she refused to give up on herself. She knew she deserved a better life. She deserved to enjoy a pain-free life.

Because she kept a positive, hopeful mindset of *never giving up,* she is still enjoying a pain-free life.

Takeaways from Mia

Having the right advice, strategies, tactics, treatment options, nutritional guidance, fitness regimens, and all the essential elements for a healthy, pain-free, energized, and vibrant life is a crucial foundation. However, what holds it all together is your *willpower*. Do you possess a positive, determined, and tenacious mindset?

In the face of challenges, can you persevere and keep going when things get tough? Undoubtedly, there will be days, perhaps even weeks, when you *feel* the temptation to give up. Times when progress seems elusive, and the journey becomes difficult and frustrating. *Keep going.*

Consistency is the key. It's the universal truth for anything in life, isn't it? Consistency is what transforms these new and healthy habits into ingrained routines.

Remember, lasting change does not happen overnight. It's a gradual process that demands your commitment and resilience. During those moments of doubt or difficulty, when the path seems unclear, remind yourself that you can do this. Your journey towards a healthier, more vibrant life is a testament to your strength and determination.

So, when faced with challenges, draw upon your willpower, stay consistent, and keep moving forward. The transformation you seek is within your grasp, and every step you take is a stride towards a better, more fulfilling version of yourself. Embrace the journey, celebrate your progress, and know that you have the power to achieve the vibrant and energized life you envision.

You CAN do this!

Self-Discovery: Conquer

There are plenty of excuses we all make to give up on things.

Your excuses will undermine your progress. Right now, I want you to uncover your excuses.

What are the excuses you tell yourself every day to justify giving up or not even trying something new?

Writing a list like this creates awareness of all the times you've tried to settle. Being aware of these excuses, you will become more conscious of when they try to sneak into your mind. They'll be less of a passing thought. Understand how these excuses might affect you. Then, decide to make a change.

When these excuses arise, you have to love yourself enough to raise your standards. *Never settle.* Instead, say:

"I am better than my excuses."

"I deserve to reach my goals and be happy."

"My excuses are a test. I refuse to fail."

"I love myself and I want to make myself proud."

Then, take those excuses and mentally kick them to the curb.

"Ba-bye!"

Learn to never say, "I can't." Instead, say, "I can." Remind yourself that you *are capable*. Also, be good to yourself and give yourself a break from any high expectations you have. Great accomplishments take time. But you absolutely *can* win, even if you feel like you are losing in the moment.

Let's face it, *you do not truly fail unless you quit*. But, if you pick yourself up and keep moving, *you can succeed!*

All those thoughts in our heads may tell us that we cannot succeed or that we aren't capable enough. These are the demons in our minds that *we* create. One of those demons is fear. Confront your fears head-on. Understand that fear is self-inflicted and all in the mind. If you let it, it will control you.

Get rid of anything that's holding you back. By understanding what's holding you back, you can learn how to overcome it, which ultimately takes its power away.

Whatever you tell yourself that keeps holding you back, turn it into something positive that motivates you. Make sure you have written down the reasons why you're working towards your deeply meaningful goals! Anytime you're faced with challenges or moments when you feel like giving up, read this list as a gentle reminder to help you refocus. As your reasons 'why' evolve, keep updating your list.

There is endless power in staying focused on what's truly important to you and believing in yourself.

Get Comfortable with The Uncomfortable

Putting forth effort to reach your meaningful goals is going to be uncomfortable at times. Embrace this. It will be okay.

Give yourself every opportunity to succeed. At the end of the day, when you give it your best effort, you will still be improving your overall health. There is simply no question about it. Small, healthy habits done consistently are what will help you achieve anything in life.

And, know that I am incredibly proud of you! What an awesome journey this has been.

Thank you for allowing me to be a part of your health journey. I truly feel tremendously honored and blessed to be a part of it.

Continue to be absolutely *amazing* and *beautiful*.

Final Thoughts

"Every new beginning comes from some other beginning's end."
— Seneca

What an amazing journey this has been. I'm so proud of you for taking the time to complete this book! If put to action, these steps will literally change the way you think, plan, and act, enabling you to live a sustainable, healthier lifestyle.

I do understand that change is never easy.

It requires not just the *desire* to do something different in your life, but the belief that you *can* accomplish it.

When you started this book, you were different. No question about it. There's an old Native American saying that goes something like: *You never put your foot into the same river twice.*

Think about it. When you step into a river, you *immediately* change the structure of that riverbed. Additionally, the currents are constantly shifting the dirt and rocks around. It's no longer the same river.

Every experience you have in life changes and shapes you in some way. Sometimes for the better. Sometimes not. But remember, *we evolve with every experience.*

Take Some Time

Right now, I want you to take some time for yourself.

Don't worry about the details of your new health goals you've been waiting to tackle.

There's a lot to process here. While you've already been processing some of the information and insights I've revealed to you as you've read each chapter, your mind still requires time to absorb everything.

Comparatively, when you consume a nutrient-dense meal, those nutrients don't immediately start affecting your body. First, they have to be absorbed into your bloodstream, carried throughout your body, and delivered to the places where your brain tells the rest of your circulatory system they need to be right then.

Those organs, tissues, muscles, and joints take what you've supplied and begin using it. That is when the change takes place.

Think of this book as your nutrient-dense meal. Just like your body needs time to absorb nutrients, your mind needs time to absorb the insights here. Give yourself the gift of patience, allowing the ideas within the pages to integrate into the fabric of your life, influencing not only your daily decisions but also nurturing your spirit. That's when the real magic happens – it's not just about reading, it's about making these ideas a living part of your world.

Embrace the process.

Everything is a process, but we're often in too big a hurry to change. We can get so caught up in what *will* happen, that we miss what is actually happening.

What's Happening Now?

Like that river, you are changing. You are learning, building confidence and focus, and understanding your purpose – the "*why*" of all of this. You are beginning to connect meaning to your desire for improving your health.

Something compelled you to purchase this book and start reading it. For most of you, it was probably partly an internal decision, but also externally motivated.

Now, you understand what *is* possible. Nothing you have read involves an overwhelmingly complex way of thinking. In fact, some of this is common sense, and some of the advice offers insight you've probably heard before.

Once you understand what it takes to be successful, though, that knowledge turns into power. It will give you a newfound sense of confidence and ability, knowing that *you...can...do...this.*

Before, you may not have believed in yourself or your ability. You may have lost hope that you could shed the extra pounds and change decades of unhealthy habits. But *now* you see it isn't just possible ... it *is* your inevitable future.

Why? Because, *YOU have the power to make it happen.*

Don't waste another day feeling like less than your true self.

Rediscover your inner strength so you can live the healthy, confident life you deserve.

You are worth it.

A Journey of a Thousand Miles

An ancient Chinese proverbs states: *The journey of a thousand miles begins with one step.*

That first step is crucial and it can also be life-changing.

Once you get started, the journey will test you. Temptations will hit you. This is normal, and you are not alone.

Once you have started on your journey, you may feel like giving up. This feeling is strongest in the beginning. Even if you give in to temptation, you can get right back on track.

Don't worry about what *might* happen. Don't think about how you *could* fall short. In the beginning, simply focus on simply putting one foot in front of the other.

Also, remember that your ultimate goal is only a distraction. Focus on the process, not the destination. Enjoy the ride.

Someday, when you have reached your health goals, you are going to look back and be overwhelmed with pride in what you were able to achieve. More importantly, you're going to inspire others to follow in your steps.

You are extraordinary.

We Are a Community

"Knowledge is power, community is strength and positive attitude is everything." — Lance Armstrong

We are humans and meant to be connected. We are drawn to people with common interests. However, in the deep submersion of your life and routine, there may be times when you feel alone.

You are never alone. Never.

Let's all come together and lift one another up. Let's celebrate our successes and be there for each other when we need it most.

Let's stay connected!

Instagram: *@reneejmacgregor*

Please write a review on Amazon. I appreciate your honest feedback and your time. Thank you very much!

Keep me updated on your progress!

Remember, it is about progress, *not* perfection.

Check out these expert-guided options and wellness freebies all on ReneeMacGregor.com!

Join the Weight Loss Community:

Private One-on-One Opportunities:

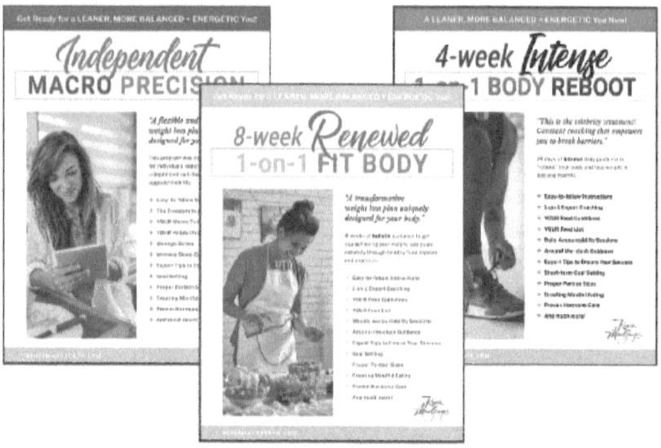

FREE Downloads at reneemacgregor.com:

Renée MacGregor
©2024

References

[1]Obesity is a Common, Serious, and Costly Disease. *Centers for Disease Control and Prevention*, July 20, 2022. https://www.cdc.gov/obesity/data/adult.html.

[2]Kelly, James. "Learning Pyramid" *The Peak Performance Center*, Sept. 2012, https://thepeakperformancecenter.com/educational-learning/learning/principles-of-learning/learning-pyramid.

[3]Dodd, Carly. "Effects of Earthquakes." *WorldAtlas*, Jan. 2021, www.worldatlas.com/articles/10-ways-an-earthquake-can-alter-the-geography-of-a-place.html#h_88654671121281610968699740.

[4]Menstrual Cramps - Symptoms & causes - Mayo Clinic. *Mayo Clinic*, April 30, 2022. https://www.mayoclinic.org/diseases-conditions/menstrual-cramps/symptoms-causes/syc-20374938.

[5]World Health Organization: WHO. Global Cancer Observatory: Cancer today. *www.who.int*, February 2021. https://gco.iarc.fr/today/online-analysis-map.

[6]"Cancer Facts & Figures 2023." *American Cancer Society*, January 24, 2023. https://www.cancer.org/content/dam/cancer-org/research/cancer-facts-and-statistics/annual-cancer-facts-and-figures/2023/2023-cancer-facts-and-figures.pdf.

[7]"Survival Rates for Bladder Cancer." *American Cancer Society*, March 1, 2023. https://www.cancer.org/cancer/types/bladder-cancer/detection-diagnosis-staging/survival-rates.html.

[8]"Survival Rates for Bone Cancer." *American Cancer Society*, March 1, 2023. https://www.cancer.org/cancer/types/bone-cancer/detection-diagnosis-staging/survival-statistics.html.

[9]"Survival Rates for Breast Cancer." *American Cancer Society*, March 1, 2023. https://www.cancer.org/cancer/types/breast-cancer/understanding-a-breast-cancer-diagnosis/breast-cancer-survival-rates.html.

[10]"Survival Rates for Cervical Cancer." *American Cancer Society*, March 1, 2023. https://www.cancer.org/cancer/types/cervical-cancer/detection-diagnosis-staging/survival.html.

[11]"Survival Rates for Colon Cancer." *American Cancer Society*, March 1, 2023. https://www.cancer.org/cancer/types/colon-rectal-cancer/detection-diagnosis-staging/survival-rates.html.

[12]"Survival Rates for Kidney Cancer." *American Cancer Society*, March 1, 2023. https://www.cancer.org/cancer/types/kidney-cancer/detection-diagnosis-staging/survival-rates.html.

[13]"Survival Rates for Liver Cancer." *American Cancer Society*, March 1, 2023. https://www.cancer.org/cancer/types/liver-cancer/detection-diagnosis-staging/survival-rates.html.

[14]"Survival Rates for Lung Cancer." *American Cancer Society*, March 1, 2023. https://www.cancer.org/cancer/types/lung-cancer/detection-diagnosis-staging/survival-rates.html.

[15]"Survival Rates for Pancreatic Cancer." *American Cancer Society*, March 1, 2023. https://www.cancer.org/cancer/types/pancreatic-cancer/detection-diagnosis-staging/survival-rates.html.

[16]"Survival Rates for Prostate Cancer." *American Cancer Society*, March 1, 2023. https://www.cancer.org/cancer/types/prostate-cancer/detection-diagnosis-staging/survival-rates.html.

[17]"Survival Rates for Thyroid Cancer." *American Cancer Society*, March 1, 2023. https://www.cancer.org/cancer/types/thyroid-cancer/detection-diagnosis-staging/survival-rates.html.

[18]Hill, Napoleon. *Think and Grow Rich*. Penguin Books Ltd., 2003. (Pg. 46, 55, 261, 279-284)

[19]Sympathetic Nervous System (SNS). *Cleveland Clinic.* https://my.clevelandclinic.org/health/body/23262-sympathetic-nervous-system-sns-fight-or-flight.

[20]Evans, O.G. "Sympathetic Nervous System: Functions & Examples." *Simply Psychology*, July 2023. https://www.simplypsychology.org/sympathetic-nervous-system.html.

[21]"Sympathetic vs. Parasympathetic Nervous System." Biology Dictionary, *Biologydictionary.net*, February 20, 2021. https://biologydictionary.net/sympathetic-vs-parasympathetic-nervous-system/.

[22]"Parasympathetic Nervous System (PNS)." Body Systems & Organs Health Library. *Cleveland Clinic*, June 6, 2022. https://my.clevelandclinic.org/health/body/23266-parasympathetic-nervous-system-psns.

[23]Evans, Olivia Guy. "Parasympathetic Nervous System (PSNS): Functions & Division." Biopsychology Theories, *Simply Psychology*, February 9, 2023. https://www.simplypsychology.org/parasympathetic-nervous-system.html.

[24]"How Many Ads Do People See in a Day 2021?" *Advertising Row Magazine*, April 5, 2022, https://advertisingrow.com/advertising-magazine/how-many-ads-do-people-see-in-a-day-2021/.

[25]Navarro, J. G. "Advertising in the United States - Statistics & Facts." Advertising & Marketing, *Statista Inc.*, May 16, 2023, https://www.statista.com/topics/979/advertising-in-the-us/#topicOverview.

[26]Navarro, J. G. "Advertising Worldwide - Statistics & Facts." Advertising & Marketing, *Statista Inc.*, May 16, 2023, https://www.statista.com/topics/990/global-advertising-market/#topicOverview.

[27]"Energy Balance" graphic. Adapted from Alan Aragon's scale, *alanargon.com.* 2019. Precisionnutrition.com

[28]Debras, Charlotte et al. "Total and Added Sugar Intakes, Sugar Types, and Cancer Risk: Results from the Prospective NutriNet-Santé Cohort." *The American Journal of Clinical Nutrition* Vol. 112,5 (Nov. 11, 2020): 1267-1279. doi:10.1093/ajcn/nqaa246.

[29]"How Much Sugar is Too Much?" Eat Smart. *American Heart Association.* (n.d.). https://www.heart.org/en/healthy-living/healthy-eating/eat-smart/sugar/how-much-sugar-is-too-much.

[30]"I Thought About Quitting, but Then I Noticed Who was Watching" graphic. Billionaire Quotes, *billionairequotess.blogspot.com.* 2018. https://billionairesquotess.blogspot.com/2018/11/i-thought-about-quitting-but-then-i.html.

[31]Norcross, J. C., Mrykalo, M. S., & Blagys, M. D. "Auld Lang Syne: Success Predictors, Change Processes, and Self-Reported Outcomes of New Year's Resolvers and Nonresolvers." *Journal of Clinical Psychology.* (2002) 58(4), 397-405. doi:10.1002/jclp.1151.

[32]Lee, Susie. "Why People Give Up" graphic. Living Your Best, *Livingyourbest.net.* 2015. https://livingyourbest.net/2015/05/12/reasons-why-people-give-up/.

[33]Bonn, Jason and Bowman, Alisa. "The Fat Loss X-factor: Learn the Lifestyle Coaching Technique that Drives Better Client Results." *Precisionnutrition.com.* (n.d.). https://www.precisionnutrition.com/can-stress-prevent-weight-loss.

[34]Williamson, Anna. "Are You Coping? Take the Stress Test." Life and Style: Stress and Anxiety: A User's Guide, Health & Wellbeing. *Theguardian.com.* February 2, 2019. https://www.theguardian.com/lifeandstyle/2019/feb/02/quiz-test-your-stress.

[35]Glickman, G., Levin, R., & Brainard, G. C. (2002). "Ocular Input for Human Melatonin Regulation: Relevance to Breast Cancer." *Neuroendocrinology Letters*, 23(Suppl 2), 17-22.

[36]Scott-Dixon, Krista et al. "The Essentials of Nutrition and Coaching for Health, Fitness, and Sport: Unit 2 Water and Food Balance." Exodus Graphics Corp. *Precisionnutrition.com.* 2019. Pg. 205.

[37]Wood, Kelly and Johnson, Jon. "How Can I Balance my Hormones?" *Medical News Today*, May 21, 2021, Article 324031. https://www.medicalnewstoday.com/articles/324031.

[38]Pandas, Sassy. "Warning: Due to Influence of Hormones I Could Burst into Tears or Kill You in the Next 5 Minutes" graphic. Sarcastic Quotes, *Pinterest.com.* (n.d.). https://www.pinterest.com/pin/pinterest--195836283784892810/.

[39]Shi, Z., Araujo, A.B., Martin, S., O'Loughlin, P., Wittert, G. "Longitudinal Changes in Testosterone Over Five Years in Community-Dwelling Men." *The Journal of Clinical Endocrinology and Metabolism.* 2013;98(8):3289-3297. doi:10.1210/jc.2012-3842

[40]Feldman, H.A., Longcope, C., Derby, C.A., et al. "Age Trends in the Level of Serum Testosterone and Other Hormones in Middle-Aged Men: Longitudinal Results from the Massachusetts Male Aging Study." *The Journal of Clinical Endocrinology and Metabolism.* 2002;87(2):589-598. doi:10.1210/jcem.87.2.8201

[41]Ley, S.H., Li, Y., Tobias, D.K., et al. "Duration of Reproductive Life Span, Age at Menarche, and Age at Menopause are Associated with Risk of Cardiovascular Disease in Women." *Journal of the American Heart Association.* 2017;6(11). doi:10.1161/jaha.117.006713

[42]Greendale, G.A., Sternfeld, B., Huang, M.H., et al. "Changes in Body Composition and Weight During the Menopause Transition." *JCI Insight*. 2019;4(5). doi:10.1172/jci.insight.124865

[43]*Institute of Health Metrics and Evaluation.* Global Health Data Exchange (GHDx). (Accessed June 23, 2023). https://vizhub.healthdata.org/gbd-results.

[44]"Caring for Your Mental Health." Mental Health Information. *National Institute of Mental Health*, December 2022. https://www.nimh.nih.gov/health/topics/caring-for-your-mental-health.

[45]Riggio, Ronald E. "10 Positive Emotions That Make Us Good People." Emotions. *Psychology Today,* August 15, 2023. https://www.psychologytoday.com/us/blog/cutting-edge-leadership/202308/the-top-10-positive-emotions-that-make-us-good-humans

[46]"Physical Wellness Checklist." Your Healthiest Self. *National Institutes of Health*, December 8, 2022. https://www.nih.gov/health-information/physical-wellness-toolkit.

[47]"Emotional Wellness Checklist." Your Healthiest Self. *National Institutes of Health*, August 8, 2022. https://www.nih.gov/health-information/emotional-wellness-toolkit.

[48]"Social Wellness Checklist." Your Healthiest Self. *National Institutes of Health*, August 26, 2021. https://www.nih.gov/health-information/social-wellness-toolkit.

[49]"Environmental Wellness Checklist." Your Healthiest Self. *National Institutes of Health*, July 21, 2022. https://www.nih.gov/health-information/environmental-wellness-toolkit.

[50]Frappier, J., Toupin, I., Levy, J.J., Aubertin-Leheudre, M., Karelis, A.D. (2013) "Energy Expenditure during Sexual Activity in Young Healthy Couples." *PLOS ONE* 8(10): e79342. https://doi.org/10.1371/journal.pone.0079342.

[51]Lehmiller, Justin J. "How Many Calories Does Sex Actually Burn? The Typical Exertion Required for Sex is Similar to Light Jogging or Swimming." Sex. *Psychology Today.* April 5, 2022. https://www.psychologytoday.com/za/blog/the-myths-sex/202204/how-many-calories-does-sex-actually-burn.

[52]Tate, Karl. "Infographic: How Many Calories Am I Burning?" *LiveScience.com*, October 17, 2013, https://www.livescience.com/40524-how-many-calories-am-i-burning-infographic.html.

[53]Tsao CW, Aday AW, Almarzooq ZI, Anderson CAM, Arora P, Avery CL, Baker-Smith CM, Beaton AZ, Boehme AK, Buxton AE, Commodore Mensah Y, Elkind MSV, Evenson KR, Eze-Nliam C, Fugar S, Generoso G, Heard DG, Hiremath S, Ho JE, Kalani R, Kazi DS, Ko D, Levine DA, Liu J, Ma J, Magnani JW, Michos ED, Mussolino ME, Navaneethan SD, Parikh NI, Poudel R, Rezk-Hanna M, Roth GA, Shah NS, St-Onge M-P, Thacker EL, Virani SS, Voeks JH, Wang N-Y, Wong ND, Wong SS, Yaffe K, Martin SS; on behalf of the American Heart Association Council on Epidemiology and Prevention Statistics Committee and Stroke Statistics Subcommittee. Heart disease and stroke statistics—2023 update: a report from the American Heart Association [published ahead of print January 25, 2023]. *Circulation.* doi: 10.1161/CIR.0000000000001123

[54]World Health Organization: WHO. Global Cancer Observatory: Cancer today. *www.who.int*, February 11, 2021. https://www.who.int/news-room/fact-sheets/detail/cardiovascular-diseases-(cvds).

[55]"Positive Thinking: Stop Negative Self-talk to Reduce Stress." Healthy Lifestyle: Stress Management, *Mayo Clinic.* February 3, 2022. https://www.mayoclinic.org/healthy-lifestyle/stress-management/in-depth/positive-thinking/art-20043950.

[56]Davis, Tchiki. "9 Ways to Cultivate a Positive Mindset." Gratitude. *Psychology Today*, May 19, 2021. https://www.psychologytoday.com/us/blog/click-here-happiness/202105/9-ways-cultivate-positive-mindset.

[57]"10 Powerful Tips to Cultivate a Positive Mindset and Improve Your Well-being." Grow Strong Motivational. *Medium*, March 9, 2023. https://medium.com/@growstrongmotivational/10-powerful-tips-to-cultivate-a-positive-mindset-and-improve-your-well-being-9a546c8ef27.

Made in United States
Troutdale, OR
09/16/2024

22858220R00166